TWAYNE'S WORLD AUTHORS SERIES

A Survey of the World's Literature

CHINA

William R. Schultz, University of Arizona

EDITOR

Tseng P'u

TWAS 576

TSENG P'U

By PETER LI

Rutgers University

TWAYNE PUBLISHERS

A DIVISION OF G. K. HALL & CO., BOSTON

Library of Congress Cataloging in Publication Data

Li, Peter, 1935–
Tseng P'u.

(Twayne's world authors series; TWAS 576: China)
Originally presented as the author's thesis,
University of Chicago.
Bibliography: p. 140–50
Includes index.
1.   Tseng, P'u, 1871–1935.
2.   Authors, Chinese—
Biography.
PL2729.S4Z77   1980   895.1′3′4   79-26219
ISBN 0–8057–6418–6

For Y. S. and Jennifer

Contents

About the Author

Born in China and educated in the United States, Peter Li received his B.A. from the University of Washington and Ph.D. in Chinese literature from the University of Chicago. At present Associate Professor of Chinese and Comparative Literature at Rutgers University, he is a contributor to *Chinese Narrative* (Princeton University Press, 1977), *Traditional Chinese Stories* (Columbia University Press, 1978), *The Chinese Novel at the Turn of the Century* (University of Toronto Press, 1980), and co-author of *Classical Chinese Fiction* (G.K. Hall, 1978). His interests are in traditional and modern Chinese literature, inter-cultural literature and the relationship between literature and society.

Preface

Tseng P'u (1872–1935) is best known as the author of the late Ch'ing novel *Nieh-hai hua* (A Flower in an Ocean of Sin) which was published in 1905 and enthusiastically received by the reading public. However, he should not be seen only as a writer of the late Ch'ing period (1900–1911); his life spanned two epochs, the last years of the monarchy and the early years of the republic, and he was active in both. In 1929 he published his second novel *Lu Nan-tzu* which was written in the modern confessional mode. Although Tseng P'u eventually came to be known primarily as a writer, he did not intend to become one as a young man. But the changed circumstances of the times determined his future for him.

The purpose of this biographical-literary study of Tseng P'u is threefold: (1) to describe the life-history of an early modern Chinese writer, (2) to present a case study of social change, and (3) to probe the complex social and literary phenomenon of the late Ch'ing period. First, we shall look at Tseng P'u's life as an artist and a writer. We shall inquire into his background and training, examine his experiences and the sources of his inspiration, and trace the pattern of his literary career. Second, as a case study of social change, we shall pay special attention to the decisions that an intellectual living in a transitional period must make. We shall see how far he follows tradition and when he departs from it. Third, the study of an individual writer and his literary associations should shed light on the literary and social conditions at the end of the Ch'ing dynasty.

Tseng P'u came from a prosperous landowning family in Kiangsu. His father, who was a lifelong dissatisfied Second Degree holder (*chü-jen*), had hoped that his son would become a holder of the Third Degree (*chin-shih*) and a scholar-official. But he was to become neither.

Tseng P'u's literary apprenticeship began with his training in the Chinese classics which was to prepare him for the civil service examinations. But it became clear that the "unorthodox" writings, such as novels, ballads, casual notes (*pi-chi*), and poetry fascinated him more.

Nevertheless, he persevered in his classical studies and did well, at least, in the early stages of the examinations. Because of good family connections Tseng P'u was able to spend his early manhood at the capital in Peking where he mingled freely with the eminent scholars of the day. It was during these "Peking days" that Tseng P'u gathered invaluable materials for his novel. While at the capital he also undertook critical research on the literature of the Later Han period (25–220 A.D.) which occupied him for four years and culminated in a long historical bibliography of the Later Han dynasty. It was a piece of work in the highly esteemed tradition of Ch'ing "empirical" scholarship and was later formally included as a supplement to the official Later Han History. The completion of that work marked the end of his training in classical scholarship.

However, Tseng P'u's literary apprenticeship continued under a different guise. After his setback in the examinations he began to study French, at first, as a tool for entering the bureaucracy. But later, after acquiring proficiency in the language, he became interested in French literature, philosophy, and social thought. He read widely in these fields under the guidance of his friend and teacher Ch'en Chi-t'ung. This gave Tseng P'u a unique background compared to the other writers of the same period many of whom had no knowledge of another language and culture.

When Tseng P'u began writing his novel in 1904, he had already abandoned his ambition to become a scholar-official. He ventured into business in Shanghai, and then started a publishing company with a number of friends. It was while he was a publisher that a friend, Chin Sung-ts'en, sent him the first six chapters of the manuscript of *Flower*, and asked Tseng P'u if he would like to continue it. Tseng P'u jumped at the opportunity and in "one breath" finished twenty chapters. It became an immediate success. Even though he was familiar with the forms of Western fiction, Tseng P'u chose to write his novel in the traditional style, though making use of some Western literary techniques. Later he was also instrumental in launching the literary magazine *Hsiao-shuo lin* (Forest of Fiction), to which he contributed five chapters of his novel.

In the latter part of 1908, Tseng P'u abandoned his literary career and became active in politics. After the revolution in 1911, he took part in the provincial politics of Kiangsu. Perhaps it was in partial fulfillment of his former ambition to become a scholar-official. However, while in office he followed literary developments and pursued his study of French literature. He intended to write a history of French literature. Among the French writers, Victor Hugo was his favorite; he translated several of Hugo's plays and novels.

Following this period of semiliterary idleness (1908–1926), Tseng P'u returned to the literary scene. He founded a publishing company, together with a bookstore and a literary magazine, all named, *Chen Mei Shan* (Truth, Beauty, and Goodness). During this later period of his literary activity, many of Tseng P'u's translations of Victor Hugo appeared, and he tried to create about him the atmosphere of the French literary salons. He also completed his second novel, *Lu Nan-tzu*, which was an autobiographical novel and a personal confession. This second work was written in the Western style, and was a literary sensation at the time.

In the last years of his life, because of ill health he had to abstain from writing altogether. He devoted these last peaceful years of his life to cultivating flowers at his home in Ch'ang-shu, Kiangsu. On his death in 1935, the literary magazine *Yü-chou Feng* (Cosmic Wind) devoted a section to commemorate him. Among those who wrote in his honor were Hu Shih and Ts'ai Yüan-pei, two eminent men of modern China.

The historical background is also significant in our attempt to understand Tseng P'u and his time. The three periods in his life correspond to three stages in China's development in modern history: self-complacency, revolution, and search for national identity. From the 1870s to 1895, China was in a state of self-complacency. In spite of her losses on the battlefields, administrative inefficiency, and widespread corruption, the basic institutions of monarchy and the bureaucratic system were still held to be viable. There were minimal attempts at technological improvement known as the Self-Strengthening Movement but it was doomed to failure. This corresponded to Tseng P'u's period of traditional classical studies.

China's losing of the Sino-Japanese War of 1894–95 suddenly awakened her to the fact that she was in grave danger of being "carved up like a melon" by the foreign powers. Hasty attempts at reform were made, but it was too late. Unrest and frustration were too great. Revolution was in the air. Although Tseng P'u did not take an active part in the political revolution of 1911, he contributed his novel of social protest *Flower* and combatted the traditional prejudice toward fiction.

The overthrow of the Manchu dynasty in 1911 and the scathing attacks on Confucianism that followed left China in a political and ideological vacuum. Her search for an ideological program and a new political system corresponded to Tseng P'u's search for new literary values and national characteristics in literature.

Tseng P'u was caught between two worlds; the late Ch'ing world of his youth and early manhood and the iconoclastic age of his maturity and old age. His artistic sense yearned for the old world of the literati-aristocracy in Peking, but he was also attracted to the new modes of expression of the 1920s. This was the dilemma of an early modern Chinese writer like Tseng P'u who was born in one age, matured and reached old age in another, but was active in both.

This study originated as a doctoral dissertation for the Department of Far Eastern Languages and Civilizations at the University of Chicago. It was Professor Phillip A. Kuhn's course on Modern China that aroused my interest in the "crisis literature" of the late Ch'ing period (1900–1910). Then under the expert guidance and encouragement of Professor David T. Roy, I selected Tseng P'u, from a myriad of late Ch'ing writers, as the subject of my research and completed my study of his life and works.

In the course of the writing, I was very fortunate to be invited by Professor Milena Doleželová-Velingerová to present my work on Tseng P'u's novel *Nieh-hai hua* (A Flower in an Ocean of Sin) at the Conference on the Late Ch'ing Novel held at the University of Toronto in 1972. Chapter 4 of this book is an outgrowth of that paper. Subsequently the paper was incorporated into a volume entitled *The Chinese Novel at the Turn of the Century* and edited by Milena Doleželová-Velingerová. I would like to thank her and the University of Toronto Press for permission to use the material here.

Also in the course of my writing, Professor T. H. Tsien suggested that I visit Mr. Tseng Hsü-pai, the son of Tseng P'u, in Taiwan. A letter of introduction from Professor Tsien to Mr. Tseng led me into the world of the Tseng family. I would like to thank Mr. Tseng for his valuable assistance. I am also grateful to him for his support and supervision of the translation of my study of Tseng P'u into Chinese by Mr. Meng-chien Ch'en whose fine rendering was a great encouragement to me.

The thoughtful suggestions, stylistic improvements, and careful editing by Professor William Schultz have made this book a much better volume. Above all, his great forbearance on my repeated requests for more time has put me in his debt.

Preface

I would also like to thank Mrs. Helen Homiak whose efficient typing and ever-cheerful disposition have eased considerably the burden of writing and rewriting.

In spite of the able assistance, I am solely responsible for errors of fact, omission, and interpretation.

Lastly, I am much more indebted to my family, Marjorie, Jennifer, and "Popo," than I am willing to admit. Their refusal to cooperate would have made this book impossible.

PETER LI

Highland Park, N. J.

Chronology

Nieh-hai hua (A Flower in an Ocean of Sin) by Chin Sung-ts'en appeared in the *Kiangsu* magazine.

1904 Founded the *Hsiao-Shuo lin she* (Forest of Fiction Company) with his friends; his grandmother died.

1905 *Flower* by Tseng P'u was published.

1906 Lin Shu mentioned reading *Flower*.

1907 *Forest of Fiction* magazine began publication; five chapters of *Flower* appeared in *Forest of Fiction*. Ch'iu Chin executed.

1908 *Forest of Fiction* ceased publication.

1909 Joined the advisory group of the Manchu governor Tuan-fang.

1910 Took a concubine, Chang Ts'ai-luan.

1911 The Republican Revolution. Elected a member of the Kiangsu Provincial Assembly.

1912 Took a second concubine, Yü I-chu.

1913 Represented Kiangsu province at the financial minister's conference in Peking; Tseng P'u's translation of Victor Hugo's *Quatre-vingt Treize* published.

1914 Became chief of the Kiangsu Bureau of Official Enterprises.

1915 Third son, Shu-mao, born.

1916 Headed the agency for reclamation and development of Huai-nan; his translation of Hugo's *Lucrèce Borgia* published.

1917 *Flower* criticized by Hu Shih.

1918 Daughter, Te, died; fourth son, Chi-yang, born.

1919 The May Fourth Movement began.

1924 Held office of Secretary of Financial Affairs in Kiangsu for four months.

1925 Held office of Secretary of Administrative Affairs in Kiangsu for nine months.

1927 Retired from politics; founded the *Chen Mei Shan* (Truth, Beauty, and Goodness) book company with his eldest son Hsü-pai.

1928 Wrote the preface to his revised edition of *Flower*.

1929 Completed his autobiographical novel *Lu Nan-tzu*.

1930 Continued *Flower* to thirty-five chapters.

1931 Truth, Beauty, and Goodness Book Company closed.

1935 Died June 23.

CHAPTER 1

Childhood and Youth

I N 1927 at the age of fifty-five, Tseng P'u began to write his slightly
disguised autobiographical novel *Lu Nan-tzu*, which he completed two years later. In this work he described his childhood and
youth up to the age of eighteen at which time he took the examinations for the First Degree in the Chinese civil service examination
system. The writing of this autobiographical work was therapeutic. It
gave Tseng P'u the opportunity to journey back in time to relive the
experiences of his youth, and with the maturity of hindsight to
recreate the lasting impressions of those years: his happy childhood,
his bittersweet educational experience, his passionate love affair and
its tumultuous aftermath, his sitting for the examinations, and his
marriage. It also frankly revealed his emotional and intellectual conflicts.

I A Happy Family Life

In looking back on his life when almost a sexagenarian, Tseng P'u
considered himself very fortunate in spite of the hardships he had
suffered. He had witnessed China's defeat at the hands of the
Japanese in 1895 when he was twenty-two years old, and the occupation of Peking by the eight allied Western powers in 1901 as a result of
the Boxer Uprising. Then, in 1911, the Ch'ing dynasty collapsed,
ending the two-thousand-year-old monarchical system and bringing
in its wake the birth of the Chinese republic.

Tseng P'u was born in Ch'ang-shu, Kiangsu, on March 1, 1872, the
eldest and only son, and the favorite child in the Tseng household. He
was raised in a large, traditional, extended Chinese family with his
parents, grandmother, aunts, uncles, sisters, and many cousins all
under the same roof. The family also had scores of servants. He wrote
of his childhood in *Lu Nan-tzu*: *Lien* (Love):

Since Lu Nan-tzu [1] was the first son in the family and a delightful child, his
parents, Lu Kung-ming and Madam Liu, naturally loved him dearly; but his

grandmother, Matriarch Ch'i, especially treasured him like a pearl. When the wind blew she thought that he would freeze, and when the sun shone she feared that he would be burnt. After he was four years old, she had him sleep with her at night. Even after he was six and had entered school, she was still unwilling to let him sleep by himself. It was not until he was ten that the Matriarch finally permitted a separate bed to be set up alongside her own for him to sleep on.[2]

Although Tseng P'u was born in troubled times in China, he certainly was not born in uncomfortable circumstances. He grew up like a delicate young plant nourished by his parents and tended by his doting grandmother.

The Tseng family was also wealthy and accomplished. Tseng P'u continued in *Lu Nan-tzu*:

Lu Nan-tzu was born in a family with a long scholarly tradition. He was born in the town of Ch'—on the south bank of the Yangtze River where the scenery was beautiful. His father Lu Hsüan [3] was a "venerable old scholar" whose official career was stalled in the examination arena. But he was a respected figure in the community. Whenever disputes arose, as soon as he spoke the parties would listen. Therefore everyone in the town referred to him as Lu Kung-ming, Lu the Just and Wise.

He became a Second Degree holder in his thirties. Although his literary skill was well known, and his friendships reached to the "dukes and ministers," in seven or eight sittings he did not succeed in earning the coveted Third Degree. . . . His mother, Madam Ch'i, being very anxious for her son's success, purchased for him the office of Department Director in the Board of Revenue.[4] With this office, his name was on the gentry roster, and the safety of the family property was assured.

But the venerable old scholar, being proud and stubborn, refused to report for the office which he believed smelt of copper. Fortunately, by relying on the one thousand or so *mou* [5] of land which his ancestors had handed down, he could get along quite well. With his earnings, he built a very elegant garden, known throughout the city, called the Lu Garden.[6] He passed his time accompanying his mother in the garden, teaching his son, studying, and enjoying his leisurely prosperity. When the time came for the Third Degree examinations, he would routinely head for the capital where he would sometimes remain for a year or two just to wait for another examination. He was not concerned about fame and glory, but he had to go through the motions for his mother who cherished the dream that one day her son would become a *chuang-yüan* or prime minister.[7]

We may pause here to explain that the *chuang-yüan* was the highest honor that anyone could achieve in traditional China through the examination system. The *chuang-yüan* was the winner of the most prestigious Palace Examination where the emperor himself selected the examination questions. And it was the dream of every parent that his or her child would distinguish himself by becoming a *chuang-yüan* and then be appointed to the office of prime minister (*tsai-hsiang*).[8]

Tseng P'u's family had lived in Ch'ang-shu, the beautiful walled city, also enclosing her sister city of Chao-wen, for the past eight hundred years, ever since the Southern Sung dynasty (1127–1278), glorifying the family name with generals, scholars, and ministers.[9] With some 160 acres of fertile delta land, the Tseng family was comfortably off. Although Tseng P'u's father, Tseng Chih-chuan (d. 1896), did not hold high office or enhance the family fortune, he was a distinguished essayist in his own right and highly regarded by his contemporaries, many of whom held high office in Peking.[10]

Tseng P'u's father was a typical traditional man of letters, a scholarly gentleman skilled in medicine, who was not particularly ambitious, and who was not interested in modernization during a time of intense contact with the West. He was a gentle, good-natured man, and frequently casually dressed. Tseng P'u was very close to him; there was not the usual antagonism between father and son. Tseng P'u gives us this description:

Lu Kung-ming . . . was of average build and had a round face with a sparse mustache; his eyes were kind and sincere. He was somewhat careless about his dress, either a button was unbuttoned or his trouser string was unfastened. The ends would dangle, one long and one short. He often held a snuff box in his hand, and he would sniff continuously, at the same time pacing back and forth with his head bent down deep in thought. At other times, he would sit quietly lost in thought with his head thrown back. One knew at a glance that this was a scholar! [11]

This intimate sketch of his father captured the essence of the leisurely Chinese gentleman-scholar.

II *Early Schooling*

Although Tseng P'u began his education at the age of six, he was not a particularly good pupil and did not enjoy his studies. He was an intelligent child, but he was also mischievous. He had a good memory and good powers of understanding, but he was easily distracted.

According to *Lu Nan-tzu*, studying the Confucian classics was like pulling teeth:

> When he studied the *Great Learning* and the *Doctrine of the Mean*, he merely imitated the chanting of the teacher; he was not actually reading, he just sang. When he studied the *Analects* of Confucius and the *Mencius*, he was bored. Later when the texts were changed to the *Book of Changes* and the *Book of History*, the more he read the less he understood. Not only was he disgusted with the whole thing, but he became resentful and angry. He refused to follow mindlessly like a parrot. Because of this, he suffered the teacher's scolding and beating no one knows how many times. He was not beaten with a ruler or with the hand; it was with anything that the teacher had in his hand at the time, and it was applied to the student's head. Sometimes the teacher pulled on the student's ear until it dripped blood. At other times, he held the hot metal tip of his long pipe against his student's head.[12]

This may sound cruel according to present-day standards, but it was the common practice in Tseng P'u's time. It was the customary ritual which the children of all scholarly families had to go through. Learning the Confucian classics was foremost in achieving success in traditional Chinese society. The nine canonical works of Confucianism were made up of the Four Books and Five Classics. The Four Books include the *Great Learning, Doctrine of the Mean, Analects,* and *Mencius.* The Five Classics include the more difficult *Book of Changes, Book of History, Book of Poetry, Book of Rites,* and *Spring and Autumn Annals.* These books were to be committed to memory as early as possible so that the student would be prepared to sit for the examinations.

Tseng P'u was not a precocious child, and he detested learning the classics. Although his parents were usually indulgent in other matters, when it came to his education they were ruthlessly strict. No one objected to the teacher's brutal methods, except Tseng P'u's grandmother who would once in a while intercede on his behalf. But Tseng P'u's mother was particularly harsh. The more she was concerned about her son's success, the stricter she became. She always sat in a room adjacent to her son's study. Through a crack in the double-leafed door which separated the two rooms, she watched and listened to her son's recitation of his lessons. When she heard his voice drop, she would pound on the door a few times to spur him on. He would then raise his voice and begin again. "This pounding and raising and lowering of the voice were repeated who knows how many times a day."

Tseng P'u's childhood days, however, did not consist entirely of this unpleasant recitation of the classics. Often his grandmother treated him to stories and chanted ballads (*t'an-tz'u*)—a popular form of storytelling in which verse was interspersed with prose—said to appeal to the common people, especially women and children. Tseng P'u wrote:

At this time Lu Nan-tzu's only suffering was study, and his only joy was listening to storytelling. Every day after school he accompanied his grandmother to supper, and usually afterwards she would chant ballads or recite episodes from famous novels. Lu Nan-tzu was extremely empathetic when stories from the *Biography of Yüeh Fei* were told; he would identify with the famous Sung general Yüeh Fei (1103–1141). When stories from the *Pacification of the East* were told, he would identify with the famous T'ang general Hsüeh Jen-kuei (612-681). He would identify with Tso Wei-ming from the ballad *Heavenly Flower*, and Chao An from *Pacification of the State.*[13]

Tseng P'u enjoyed listening to these stories purely for pleasure, but they served a double purpose of entertainment and moral indoctrination. These novels and ballads were extremely popular and they combined powerful moral lessons on patriotism, filial piety, righteousness, and integrity with fascinating supernatural adventures and grand feats of bravery and heroism by great generals, warriors, and men of letters.

Since these works were important to Tseng P'u, let us examine them briefly. *Shuo Yüeh ch'üan chuan* (The Biography of Yüeh Fei), by the early eighteenth-century writer Ch'ien Ts'ai, is a heavily romanticized account of the great patriot and general Yüeh Fei. He was the archetypal tragic hero who gave his life to his country and whose brilliant military career was cut short due to the machinations of evil ministers at the emperor's court. *Cheng-tung* (Pacification of the East) is a highly popular and fictionalized military romance about the adventures of the T'ang general Hsüeh Jen-kuei in his conquest of Korea and his romances with barbarian princesses. *T'ien yü-hua* (Heavenly Flower) is a ballad attributed to a nineteenth-century woman writer, T'ao Chen-huai. It tells of the patriotic efforts of a man of letters, Tso Wei-ming, and his daughter Tso I-cheng to save the failing Ming dynasty (1368–1644). When all their attempts end in futility, they commit suicide. *An-pang-chih* (Pacification of the State), an early nineteenth-century work, is the first of a trilogy of ballads about the founding of the Sung dynasty (960–1278) by members of the Chao family. These are all exciting works that could easily capture the child's imagination. Since these early sessions of ballad chantings were Tseng P'u's first introduction to popular Chinese literature, they may well have influenced his later literary development.

At first these recitations by his grandmother fascinated him, but soon afterward he wanted to read the stories for himself. He ventured into his grandmother's room and without any difficulty took a few ballad texts, among them *Lai sheng fu* (Happiness in the Next Life). It is a ballad about Liu Ch'un-hui, the hero, whose utmost filiality causes him to request that upon his death he be reincarnated as the child of his former parents so that he may fulfill his filial duty to them. Tseng P'u read these ballads whenever he had a spare moment.

After he became tired of these ballads, he advanced to traditional vernacular fiction, such as *Feng-shen pang* (Investiture of the Gods),[14] *Tung-Chou lieh-kuo chih* (A History of the States of the Eastern Chou),[15] *Hsi yu chi* (*Journey to the West*),[16] and *Ching hua yüan* (*Flowers in the Mirror*).[17] Then he read the semiliterary historical novel *San-kuo yen-i* (*The Romance of the Three Kingdoms*).[18] At this point he exhausted his grandmother's library.

Next, Tseng P'u explored his father's collection. There he found *Hung-lou meng* (*The Dream of the Red Chamber*), China's greatest novel and a masterpiece of world literature.[19] Tseng P'u's "joy was probably greater than Columbus's joy upon discovering the New World." *Dream* opened up new vistas: the many beautiful maidens and the delicate, romantic, temperamental young hero Chia Pao-yü pleased him greatly. He must have identified easily with Pao-yü. Whereas before he had read novels only when he had a spare moment, now he read *Dream* even when he should have been studying. He could not bear to leave it behind. "Before, he was only interested in the physical prowess of the martial heroes, but now his interests turned toward the fair sex . . . he suddenly realized that there was an entirely different way of life."

Tseng P'u's new literary ventures led him to the eighteenth-century novel of erudition with passages of eroticism, *Yeh-sou p'u-yen* (A Rustic's Idle Talk)[20] which he discovered in his father's library. Unfortunately, this time he was found out. His usually mild-mannered father burst out in anger. His face turned blood-red, and pounding on the table with his fist, he gave his son a sound scolding. Then he ransacked Tseng P'u's study, taking away all the books not belonging to him. His grandmother was also asked to lock up her bookcase so that her wayward grandson would not have access to her books, either.

Tseng P'u was miserable for a few days after this incident. But his nature was resilient; a little later he recovered his enthusiasm and began to search for new channels. With the help of his cousins, he began to explore his uncle's library. There he found *Fei-yen wai-chuan* (The Biography of Chao Fei-yen), *Tsa-shih mi-hsin* (Miscellaneous Secret Records), and *Sou-shen chi* (Search for the Gods) from *Han-Wei ts'ung-shu* (Collectanea of the Han and Wei Dynasties).[21] The first is a fictionalized biography of the famous delicate and willowy beauty, Chao Fei-yen, who became the empress of the Han Emperor Ch'eng (r. 32–6 B.C.).[22] *Tsa-shih mi-hsin* is an erotic account of the search for a concubine for Emperor Huan (r. 136–167).[23] *Sou-shen chi* is a fourth-century work which contains a large number of ghost stories and supernatural events.[24] These stories of the strange and unusual fascinated the young Tseng P'u.

He also discovered the highly unorthodox works of the first-century philosopher Wang Ch'ung (27–97? A.D.). He read with relish the sections entitled "Questioning Confucius" and "Attacking Mencius" from Wang's *Lun-heng* (*Discourses*).[25] These works stimulated Tseng P'u's intellectual curiosity.

Tseng P'u's early literary education brought him into contact with a broad corpus of traditional Chinese literature, from the popular long narrative ballads chanted by his grandmother to the heretical discourses of the Han philosopher Wang Ch'ung. It is important to stress that Tseng P'u's first exposure to Chinese popular fiction was through the live presentation of ballads, a highly emotional and dramatic genre. His reading of traditional vernacular novels on the sly was a common enough practice among children of all times in China, but his fascination with *The Dream of the Red Chamber* at the age of eleven or twelve may have been unusual. With this impressive gallery of literary personalities from ballads and novels, Tseng P'u created these romantic childhood fantasies:

First, he wished that he could become a great official skilled with the pen and the sword. At least he should be the equal of Tso Wei-ming, the hero of *Heavenly Flower*, or Liu Ch'un-hui, the hero of *Happiness in the Next Life*. Second, he wanted to become a great writer in the literary world, at least the equal of To Chiu-kung, the seasoned traveler and guide in *Flowers in the Mirror*, or Ni Cheng-p'ing, the fearless eccentric and minor character in *The Romance of the Three Kingdoms*. Third, he wanted to be pursued by many fair young maidens, whereas he himself already had his ideal beloved. . . . he had truly become a storybook character.[26]

Tseng P'u had a rich imagination; his political, scholarly, and romantic aspirations were essential ingredients for his later career as a writer.

Although Tseng P'u did not apply himself diligently to the practice of writing examination essays, much to the consternation of his father, he did show talent in other literary forms. At the age of thirteen or fourteen, his father discovered a beautifully written piece of parallel prose in his son's desk. This led him to cry out excitedly, "Ta-ta has finally done it!" (Ta-ta was Tseng P'u's nickname). And soon his literary talent was known throughout the district. It was also about this time that Tseng P'u fell passionately in love with his cousin, a Miss Ting, who became his "ideal beloved."

III   *Romance and Tragedy*

Tseng P'u's beloved was a maternal cousin whom he called familiarly "second sister Ting." She was a year older than Tseng P'u and the favorite grandniece of Matriarch Ting, Tseng P'u's grandmother. Tseng P'u came to know his cousin, Miss Ting, when they were still youngsters, and probably they met under these circumstances as described in *Lu Nan-tzu*:

Every New Year's, Matriarch Ch'i went back to visit her family in the country. Whenever she went she always took Lu Nan-tzu with her, and sometimes stayed as long as a month. Most of the time she would stay with Ch'i Han-chiang and his family; and whenever the Ch'i family came to the city, they would stay with the Lu's. Although Lu Nan-tzu and Miss Ch'i were distant cousins, they were very close since they had known each other since childhood. Whenever they met, they would stick together like candy. When the adults saw them together, they would point with amusement and say jokingly, "Don't they look like a little couple?" [27]

In this passage, of course, Miss Ch'i is in fact Tseng P'u's cousin, Miss Ting. Thus, Tseng P'u's relationship with his cousin, which began as an innocent childhood friendship, blossomed later into full-fledged love. Cousin romances of this kind were not uncommon among children of large families in China.

On another occasion, they saw a good deal of each other. When Miss Ting's family had a new house built, the Tings came to stay with Tseng P'u's family for half a year. But this association was not an unmixed blessing because Tseng P'u had strong sexual desires. He was very much in love with his cousin, but he had to respect her wish that their relationship remain pure. He revealed this conflict in his diary of May 25, 1928:

> When I was a young man, I was filled with feelings and emotions, and I had strong sexual desires. In my romance with T, it was only because I respected her wishes that I kept the relationship pure and never attempted to violate her. This is the truth. I remember every morning and evening after we met and had our tête-á-tête, I would leave in a state of frenzy. You can imagine, at that time when my desires were rampant, and after that kind of stimulation, my whole body would burn like fire. How could I bear it? At first I relieved myself with my fingers, which I had learned from reading *The Romance of the Western Chamber*. . . . But I was still not satisfied. Slowly I began to experiment with the real thing.[28]

The diary reveals how he first seduced a maid about nineteen years old who had a round face and rosy cheeks. Then, a neighborhood girl, somewhat prettier than the first, began flirting with him, and of course, he did not reject her. Tseng P'u was sixteen at the time. Almost fifty years later he was to write regretfully that this set a pattern for his later libertine ways from which he could not restrain himself.

Tseng P'u's romance with his cousin Ting lasted until his seventeenth year when their relationship was broken because of taboos against cross-cousin marriage. Tseng P'u was heartbroken, but there was nothing he could do. The young people had no part in making these decisions. His frustration led him to further debaucheries:

> There was nothing I could do but abandon myself to dissolute ways in order to relieve my frustrations. Everything that would alleviate the desires of the flesh . . . there was none which I did not do . . . . If it had not been for my father who sent me off to Peking, there is no telling what a mess I would have made of myself.[29]

Fortunately, his father intervened and his spree of dissipation was halted. His trip to Peking was beneficial to him in more ways than one. This will be discussed further in the next chapter.

When the time came for the civil service examinations in the autumn of 1890, Tseng P'u was called back from Peking. In spite of his emotional state, he did well on this first of a series of three examinations, the district examination: he ranked number one. He placed second on the prefectual examination, the second in the series. With

one more examination to go, Tseng P'u seemed to have the First
Degree firmly within his grasp. In the meantime, Tseng P'u's father
had arranged a marriage for his son. But his bride was not his cousin
Ting. She was Wang Yüan-shan, the third daughter of Wang Ming-
luan (1838–1907), an old friend and colleague of Tseng P'u's father.
Wang was a high official in Peking and presumably this marriage
would be beneficial to Tseng P'u. Tseng P'u, however, had not
forgotten his first love. On the day of the wedding, he drank heavily
and used his drunkenness as a pretext for not entering the nuptial
chamber. But he could not long hold a grudge against the young
bride, for she had nothing to do with his unhappiness. She was kind
and gentle and within two weeks they became a very happy young
couple.

After the wedding festivities were over, Tseng P'u reported to
Soochow for the third and final provincial director-of-studies examination for the First Degree. In this examination he placed seventh
and was officially admitted as a student in the government school
system. This marked Tseng P'u's initiation into manhood in traditional Chinese society. He was eighteen years old and seemed to be
happily married.

It would appear that Tseng P'u, at this stage in his career, had the
twin blessings of a happy marriage and the first official degree. But
the trauma of the breakup of his first romance was to remain with him
for the rest of his life. Forty-seven years later, when he wrote *Lu
Nan-tzu*, he revealed the full significance of that event. Tseng P'u was
emotionally crushed by the disruption of his prospective marriage
with his cousin, unbeknownst to his parents. There was also a deeper
psychosexual conflict within him between physical and spiritual love.

On the narrative level, *Lu Nan-tzu* tells of the tragic love of two
young couples. One pair is Lu Nan-tzu and his cousin Ch'i Wan-
chung; the other is Lu Nan-tzu's childhood friend, Chu Hsiao-hsiung
and his girl friend, T'ang Yün-feng. At first, Lu Nan-tzu and Chu
Hsiao-hsiung both loved Ch'i Wan-chung; but eventually Lu Nan-tzu
gains the upper hand, and Chu Hsiao-hsiung seeks out T'ang Yün-
feng. Hsiao-hsiung and Yün-feng are, by nature, more straightforward, outspoken, and bolder than the other pair. They carry on a
torrid romance, in which they throw caution to the winds, transgress
the proper bounds of Confucian morality, and consummate their love
in sexual union. Gradually they experience guilt, remorse, and restlessness. After their affair is discovered by Yün-feng's family, they
disgrace her by excluding her from the ancestral hall. The young

couple become outcasts of their families and are ostracized by society. Finally they must pay for their transgressions with their lives. They commit suicide by taking overdoses of opium.

Lu Nan-tzu and Ch'i Wan-chung, on the other hand, are by nature more restrained, subtle, and unpredictable than the other pair. Although their relationship is full of tensions and misunderstandings, and although moments of intense joy and happiness alternate with moments of desperate jealousy and self-pity, it remains a pure, "spiritual" relationship throughout, unmarred by sex. Although their relationship has its ups and downs, they have an unquestioned understanding that they will some day be married. But fate is unkind to them. A village upstart, Wang Lu-t'ing, ruins the marriage plans. The novel ends with a long letter from Lu Nan-tzu to Wan-chung in which he asks her for forgiveness, pleads with her not to remain angry, and not to feel self-pity. He expresses his own disillusionment with love, but at the same time, he feels that disappointments are beautiful. They are the inspiration for all the arts. Here is a short excerpt:

Ever-beloved Wan, disappointment is the most beautiful feeling in life. It is depicted in all literatures. We are like two streams that flow out from the same primeval spring of life: if we were not destined to part, how could we have had the good fortune of being together? Ever-beloved Wan, do not feel heartbroken anymore; do not be resentful. We ought to regard the memory of our love as a work of art which can be cherished always. Let it remain forever in our hearts. At the final moment when we leave this world, perhaps it will still appear in our weakened vision and accompany us into our graves.[30]

Finally, he proposes that their love should be preserved as an eternal object of art.

There is no question that *Lu Nan-tzu* is a slightly disguised autobiographical work. Tseng P'u records in his diary:

Someone asked me, "Is *Lu Nan-tzu* true?"
Of course it is true. The incidents and times may be changed around, but this is the common practice among novelists who write in the autobiographical style. The important thing is that the feelings and emotions are true: thus, everywhere in the novel the feelings and emotions are all true without any exceptions. . . .[31]

Of course we cannot expect Tseng P'u to give us a facsimile account of the events of his youth. In fact, what we do have is a self-portrait with very strong romanticist tendencies of self-dramatization, piercing

self-analysis, and an excessive outflow of sentimentality. But, in spite
of these characteristics, we can identify Tseng P'u's real conflicts and
their resolution.

On the psychological level, in Chu Hsiao-hsiung, Tseng P'u has
created his alter ego, who is the bolder and more impulsive counterpart of himself. With him Tseng P'u debates the questions of love and
morality, physical versus spiritual love, and plays out alternative
courses of action. Hsiao-hsiung and Yün-feng take the step which Lu
Nan-tzu and Wan-chung refrain from taking, thus sparing the latter
couple the penalty of death. Tseng P'u has thus justified his own
spiritual love and condemned, though with his full sympathy and
understanding, the more perilous ways of physical love.

Tseng P'u has also absolved his parents from blame for arranging
his marriage with another girl instead of with his cousin. This he has
done by creating Wang Lu-t'ing, the avaricious parvenu, who under-
mines Lu Nan-tzu's chance to marry his cousin. Thus Wang Lu-t'ing
becomes the scapegoat for his parents. In the final analysis, Tseng P'u
has resolved the conflict between spiritual and physical love, reconciled himself to the prevailing morality of his time, and justified
himself for obeying his parents.

This psychoanalytic interpretation of the novel is not the only one
possible. I deal with the novel from another perspective in Chapter 3
in this book. But it is clear that Tseng P'u in this way resolved a
psychological "knot" of his early life.

Tseng P'u was a sensitive child, playful, imaginative, and passionate. In the years from 1872 to 1889, during the period of his childhood
and youth, when China was thrown open to foreign influences, Tseng
P'u led a very sheltered life with practically no contact with the
outside world, although Shanghai was only sixty miles away. His
educational training was completely traditional, uninfluenced by
Western learning. Clearly he possessed literary talent and had
showed himself to be capable of great emotional attachment. Looking
at the other side of his nature, he was not a very diligent student; he
was spoiled by his doting grandmother; he was emotional, sentimen-
tal, and sexually promiscuous. He was a romantic through and
through—in the French sense of *romanesque*. In sum, Tseng P'u had
a happy childhood and thoroughly enjoyed all the blessings of the
traditional extended family system.

CHAPTER 2

Examinations and Classical Scholarship

I   *District Examination of 1890*

IN the last chapter we had gotten slightly ahead in the narrative; let us now backtrack a bit to the time before Tseng P'u sat for the examinations. He began to prepare for the examinations in earnest at the age of twelve or thirteen when the family engaged the renowned scholar P'an Yü-jen (d. 1891) as his tutor. Five years later, in 1890, at the age of eighteen, Tseng P'u took the first in a series of examinations for the First Degree. Of course, Tseng P'u did not study diligently all this time; his teacher and elders were frequently reprimanding him for reading "frivolous" literature, such as fiction, dramas, and what-not, whenever their backs were turned. Needless to say, he was also having a love affair with his cousin, Miss Ting.

As we mentioned before, Tseng P'u was sent to Peking as a result of this love affair. But this trip to Peking turned out to be an important event for Tseng P'u; it was his first time away from home and his first exposure to the capital city. The cosmopolitanism of Peking with its "sea of scholars" inspired him to undertake serious study. For some time, Tseng P'u had wanted to compile a bibliography of writings of the Later Han dynasty (25–220), and this trip to Peking reinforced his desire. Furthermore, since critical studies in the tradition of Han scholarship were in vogue, as opposed to the speculative philosophy of the Sung and Ming, many Ch'ing scholars took Han learning as the model. Thus, to compile a historical bibliography of the works of the Later Han period was also a timely thing to do. In 1889, Tseng P'u began in his spare time to read and take notes from the *Hou-Han shu* (History of the Later Han Dynasty), *Sui shu* (History of the Sui Dynasty), and other works. Within a few months he had collected a total of over five hundred titles.[1] When the second lunar month came, Tseng P'u had to put aside his work, return home to Ch'ang-shu, and prepare himself for the examinations. This was his first test of manhood in traditional Chinese society.

A few days before the important event, friends and neighbors came to wish the candidate well. Especially close friends and relatives also came to help prepare the special examination basket by bringing food and gifts. Tseng P'u had not been a particularly diligent student, and he was not eager about the examination. But he had reconciled himself to it and began to prepare:

He quickly sat down at his desk, gathered together his paper and writing brushes, and some books with which he was most familiar and put them into a three-tiered, rectangular, fine-woven examination basket. When he saw that the ink in the ink-slab had dried to a crisp, he smiled at his own neglect. Just as he had selected a stick of pine-scented ink and began grinding, his father walked in.

"Are you preparing your examination gear?" his father asked, smiling. "Good, now you are like a child of our family."

Thereupon, father and son discussed the rules and regulations, and the various literary taboos of the examination. After lunch, an unending stream of relatives came to wish the candidate success.[2]

It might be interesting to note here that the examination basket which seems insignificant was an extremely important piece of examination equipment. Since the student was shut up in an examination cell for the whole day, the basket must contain all the comforts of home, bedding, books, medicines, food, refreshments, and all the necessary writing utensils.

On the day of the examination, Tseng P'u rose before dawn. The district examination began at the crack of dawn and lasted until sunset. The site of the examination was the city temple in the district yamen in Ch'ang-shu city itself. With the family examination basket in his hand, Tseng P'u entered the examination hall:

A formidable and awe-inspiring city temple. In the late evening of a wintry day, although there was a penetrating chill, inside the city temple starting in the main hall, along the passage way, and all the way into the inner hall, there was a mass of bobbing heads seated along narrow, wooden tables. Some of the students were hunched over writing; others leaned back deep in thought; some were chanting and rocking from side to side. In front of them were the flickering flames of the whale oil candles. . . . This was the district city temple which was being used as the examination hall.

Under the candle light, at the east side of the main hall, with some seven or eight colorful images of lictors standing behind them, sat a row of examination candidates bent over their table. Among them was one who was particularly young; although he appeared full-grown, at heart he was still a child. At the moment he was hunched over his red-lined examination booklet, hurriedly copying and writing. Suddenly he raised his tired, worried face; as if startled, he looked around him. This was Lu Nan-tzu taking his first step onto the battlefield of life.[3]

As previously mentioned, Tseng P'u did well on the district examination. In the fourth lunar month, after a month's rest, there was the prefectural examination in which Tseng P'u placed second. Between the prefectural and the final provincial director-of-studies examination was an interval of three months. Tseng P'u was married during this time. (This occasion we discussed in the last chapter.) Then he hastened to Soochow for the final part of the examination which he passed in seventh place and which earned him the First Degree. Since the government quota was generally small, only one to two percent of the total number of students who began the district examination cleared this final hurdle;[4] the passing of this examination was an achievement to be proud of.

Liang Ch'i-ch'ao (1873–1929), one of the leading intellectuals and reformers of modern China and a contemporary of Tseng P'u, gave this account of the grueling experience of the examinations:

. . . it took a month to attend the several parts of the district examination (*hsien-shih*). After a month, one attended the prefectual examination (*fu-shih*) which also took a month. After another month, one was examined by the provincial director-of-studies (*yüan-shih*). When all three sets of examinations were over, half a year had passed. When one failed, one became discouraged and could not concentrate on study for several months.[5]

II *The Provincial Examination of 1891*

After completing this first series of examinations for the First Degree, Tseng P'u went to Peking again to pursue his research projects. Aside from continuing his bibliographical study, he became acquainted with the prominent scholars and officials of his day, such as Li Wen-t'ien (1834–1895), Wen T'ing-shih (1856–1904), Chiang Piao (1860–1899), Wang Ming-luan (1837–1907), and Wu Ta-ch'eng (1835–1902). Li Wen-t'ien was the Senior Vice-President of the Board of Rites and an outstanding scholar of Mongol history. Wen T'ing-shih was an influential progressive who often advised the emperor on matters of reform. He was also an expert on Mongol history. Chiang Piao was a compiler in the prestigious Hanlin Academy. Hung Chün was the Senior Vice-President of the Board of

War and was special minister to Russia, Germany, Austria, and Holland from 1887–1890. Hung was also the first Chinese to use Western sources in the study of Mongol history. Wang Ming-luan, a Senior Vice-President of the Board of Works and a versatile scholar, later became Tseng P'u's father-in-law. Finally, Wu Ta-ch'eng was a many-sided civil and military official who was also interested in archeology and calligraphy. He held various diplomatic and military posts and was governor of Kwangtung and later of Hunan. Although these men were all senior to Tseng P'u by some ten to twenty years, they befriended him because he was a promising young scholar, and out of friendship for his father. Tseng P'u studied some Mongol history, but his stay in Peking was cut short by the Second Degree examination which was coming in the eighth lunar month. By the end of summer, Tseng P'u headed south again.

After arriving home and getting a few things together, Tseng P'u and his father sailed for Nanking, where the examination was to be held. It was fortunate that Tseng Chih-chuan accompanied his son to Nanking because midway on their journey Tseng P'u suddenly became ill. He was feverish, suffered from diarrhea and nausea, and when the boat arrived in Nanking he could hardly walk. Since Tseng P'u's father was skilled in medicine, he quickly brewed his son some medicine to relieve him of the symptoms and then sent him off to the examination hall. After entering the examination hall, Tseng P'u pulled himself together and did quite well; he was initially ranked seventeenth among all the successful candidates, but was later changed to the 101st place. According to the account given by the assistant examiner and family friend, Li Sheng-to (1860–1937), this is what happened:

The three essays which you wrote during the first session were in entirely different styles. The first was in the style of the Yün-chien school; the second was in the style of the two poets Chiang Yen (444–505) and Pao Chao (414–466) of the Six Dynasties period (420–589), and the last in the style of the illustrious Su family of the Sung. When the label was removed, revealing your place of ancestry and age, and Mr. Chin Chung-fu, the chief examiner, saw that your age was only seventeen, he cried out in alarm, "This paper must have been written by a substitute! How can a child who still smells of milk write three essays in three different styles! It would be safer to eliminate him."

At the time I remonstrated with him and was certain that the examination paper was yours. I tried to convince him not to "let a pearl slip out of the net" and thus lose a good student. But Mr. Chin was afraid of complications.

Although he promised not to eliminate your paper, he moved it from the seventeenth place to the 101st place and said with amusement, "In any case, I gave him a *first!*" [6]

At this examination there occurred one of those strange quirks of fate. Tseng P'u was set back because, first, his essays were too well written and, second, he reported his age as being too young. The falsification of age was a common practice at the time because passing the examinations was highly unpredictable. A candidate felt it safer to put down his age as being a few years younger than he actually was, so that if he should fail the examination a few times he would not be penalized. This was one of the lesser corruptions of the examination system. In Tseng P'u's case, however, this procedure backfired. In spite of the difficulties, nevertheless, he passed the provincial examination—not at seventeen but at age twenty *sui* (the Chinese reckoning), and not in the seventeenth place but in the 101st place. Seventeen was his unlucky number.

A personal tragedy occurred two months later, which was to disturb Tseng P'u greatly. Before the examination, Tseng P'u's wife, Wang Yüan-shan, was about to have a child; in the eleventh lunar month she gave birth to a baby girl. Mother and child were doing fine until the fourth day. Then the mother suddenly became ill and died two weeks later. The baby lived for two months and then died. Tseng P'u was very distressed and wrote a drama entitled *Hsüeh-t'an-meng yüan-pen* (Dream of the White T'an Flower) in memory of his wife. [7]

III *The Metropolitan Examination of 1892*

The Third Degree examination in Peking followed close upon the Second Degree examination. The provincial examination was held in the middle of the eighth lunar month and lasted for nine days; the metropolitan examination took place in the third lunar month of the following year; but the candidate must submit his name and place of ancestry to the Board of Rites by the eleventh lunar month, and must report to Peking by the tenth day of the first month. If he were late, then he would not be admitted to that year's examination and must wait three years for the next one. Therefore, despite his personal tragedy at home, Tseng P'u had to prepare himself for this final test. Even though he was reluctant to go, his parents, relatives, and friends, distant and close, all urged him not to pass up this rare opportunity of getting three degrees in three consecutive years.

Solicitous about his son, Tseng Chih-chuan saw him off to Shanghai and watched him board the steamer for Peking.

This examination illustrates the frustrations created by the inflexibility and cumbersomeness of the examination system. Even Weng T'ung-ho (1830–1904),[8] the grand old man in Peking, who was the chief examiner at this metropolitan examination found himself powerless. Even though he knew that there were time-tested, outstanding candidates in this session, he could not help them. About the best the examiner and his assistants could do was to guess the style of writing of the candidates, a well-nigh impossible task considering the hundreds of candidates taking the examinations. Weng tried to select Chang Chien (1853–1926) as the number one candidate in this examination; but a certain Liu Fu-yao was chosen instead. Chang's paper was eliminated early in the contest because of a calligraphical error.[9] Weng T'ung-ho was also on the lookout for Tseng P'u's paper. He had such confidence in his perspicacity that when the name-concealing label was about to be removed, he shouted, "This must be Tseng P'u's paper! This must be Tseng P'u's paper!" What he thought was Tseng P'u's paper was Huang Ch'ien-chai's. As it turned out, Huang was a childhood friend of Tseng P'u and they could both write in the Six Dynasties style. So Weng mistook Huang's paper for Tseng's. Unknown to Weng T'ung-ho, Tseng P'u had already disqualified himself by spilling ink over his examination booklet. He dashed off two poems in seven-syllable regulated verse and walked out. They read:

I

A young man does not begrudge the years,
Even though a literary setback brings him pains severe.
Much precious ink has been poured forth from the golden
  vessel,
But from the high tower, the arbiter with the jade
  ruler lets fall an immortal.
A blank tablet I submit, not because my talents are
  exhausted,
Rather, the sleep-laden arbiter has favored the wrong
  beauteous gem.
Flowers blossom, flowers fall, it is a common sight
  indeed,
At first they drift and scatter, that is for certain
  ordained.

II
But then wildly laughing, I grasp by Wu sword,
And think how could a heaven-endowed talent come to such
    an end?
Suddenly, without reason, I comprehend my fate,
That for me, fame and glory, are not to be sought for
    in this place.
Why does the scholar need to pursue a mistaken goal?
There is no need for me to divine whether I leave or
    stay!
Upon the morn I shall toss aside my pen and leave,
To try my noble steed at the crossing where the
    nine roads meet.[10]

The first poem expresses his disappointment at his own misfortune, and he laments his fate. He sees himself as an abandoned heavenly immortal, an undiscovered gem, and a wilted flower. In the next poem, however, he realizes that he does not have to be bound by the verdict of the examinations. There are other avenues open to him. He is ready to face the future with renewed courage.

Tseng P'u's state of mind at this point is not difficult to imagine. He had just lost his beloved wife and child. He did not want to sit for the examinations, but his father forced him to board the steamer for Peking. After entering the examination hall, on an impulse, he knocked over a bottle of ink and soiled his examination booklet. When efforts to get another booklet failed, since there was no such precedent, he dashed off two poems and left. Tseng P'u gave us this account in his reminiscences:

As for those things which followed upon the spilling of ink, such as proctor Li insisting on a precedent, and Ch'i Hsiu's coming to comfort me in my stall, these were all true. But as for vomiting blood, and Ho-some-body from Yünnan bringing me soup, and his sleeve getting caught on the ink bottle and knocking it over, these were all nonsense. They were fabrications I used to cover up my impulsive act—an uncontrollable emotional outburst. [11]

After Tseng Chih-chuan heard about his son's accident at the examination, he knew very well his son's feelings. Thereupon he purchased for him the office of Secretary of the Grand Secretariat (*nei-ko chung-shu*), with rank 7b, and told him to remain in Peking for the time being.

Tseng P'u was never to take the examinations again, nor did he, like his father, take his new office very seriously. He began his long search for a new goal in life.

IV   *Apprenticeship in Classical Scholarship*

Although during the period from 1892–96 Tseng P'u was supposed to be an official at the capital, actually he was constantly travelling back and forth between Ch'ang-shu and Peking. But these were fruitful years in Tseng P'u's life; Peking had much to offer him. The city had its own character. Peking society was different from that of his quiet home of Ch'ang-shu, and that of the bustling commercial city of Shanghai. Polite conversation was a cultivated art; Peking opera was in vogue. One could find all sorts of people in Peking: experts in every field. Scholarship was pursued for its own sake. Men of talent throughout the land came to Peking to broaden their horizons and polish their learning and manners. Even the *chuang-yüan* did not feel at ease in Peking until he had imbibed Peking culture, developed special interests, such as collecting rare books, antiques, or paintings. In short, his whole life-style changed once he lived in Peking.

In his novel *A Flower in an Ocean of Sin*, Tseng P'u describes the changes that four characters undergo when they arrive in Peking:

T'ang-ch'ing immediately pushed essay writing to the back of his mind and became interested in collecting rare books. He bought a few Sung and Yüan editions, practiced small-seal calligraphy, and studied works on etymology.

Chüeh-chai was by nature more active. For a while he painted and practiced calligraphy, and then acquired for himself the reputation of being an eccentric scholar. Then for a time he discoursed on the teachings of the Ch'eng-Chu and Lu-Wang schools of philosophy, and acted like a Neo-Confucian. He bought some old bronzes and ancient jades and became an expert on bronze and stone inscriptions. After leafing through some books on military strategy, he proclaimed himself an expert on military affairs.

For Chao-t'ing, who was already interested in poetry and literature, there was no need to say more.

Only Feng-ju was the same old pedant. He stuck to his examination essays and refused to cultivate other interests. Wen-ch'ing and the others often laughed at him, but he did not care.[12]

It might be interesting to note that two of these characters, T'ang-Ch'ing and Chüeh-chai, were, respectively, modeled on Tseng P'u's father-in-law, Wang Ming-luan, and a close family friend, Wu Ta-ch'eng, who had arranged Tseng P'u's marriage with the Wangs.

On another occasion, when these scholars were discussing famous men in Peking, the emphasis was again on the arts of calligraphy and connoisseurship:

> Kung-fang said, "Well, you cannot make sweeping judgements. In my humble opinion . . . as for calligraphy, of course Kung Ho-fu is the best. The foremost collector of bronzes and stone inscriptions is P'an Pa-ying. In the art of poetry and essay writing, Li Chih-min of K'uai-chi is the most outstanding. One possessing wide learning and prodigious knowledge, but not belonging to any particular school is Chuang Shou-hsiang of Nan-p'i, the hero of the north." [13]

The four gentlemen referred to in the passage were all veritable landmarks in Peking. Kung Ho-fu was Peking's grand old man Weng T'ung-ho; P'an Pa-ying was P'an Tsu-yin (1830–1890), President of the Board of Works and a famous collector; Li Chih-min was Li Tz'u-ming (1830–1894), a fearless, straightforward censor and prolific writer, and Chuang Shou-hsiang was Chang Chih-tung (1837–1909), governor-general of Kwangtung and Kwangsi, a man of phenomenal memory with an excellent classical education. Other men of distinction were mentioned in the text, but this is sufficient to give us an idea of the many famous men in Peking.

For four or five months after the metropolitan examinations in 1892, Tseng P'u stayed with his father-in-law, Wang Ming-luan, at his home on the east side of the great moat surrounding the Forbidden City. He rode the streets of the capital proudly with his friends, Chao Ch'un-nien, Weng Chiung-sun, and others. During this period Tseng P'u frequented the home of Hung Chün, who had only recently returned from his three-year term as ambassador to Europe, and met the wife of the ambassador, Fu Ts'ai-yün, who later became the famous entertainer Sai-chin-hua (1874–1936) and the heroine of Tseng P'u's book *A Flower in an Ocean of Sin*.

But more will be said about this later. Hung Chün died in October, 1893, and the Hung household moved away from Peking. Tseng P'u left Peking in the autumn of 1892 and did not return until the spring of 1894. It was probably in the summer of 1892 that Tseng P'u saw Hung Chün and Sai-chin-hua for the last time.

When Tseng P'u returned to Ch'ang-shu in the autumn of 1892, his father had made arrangements for him to marry Miss Shen Hsiang-sheng, the eighth daughter of Shen Chin-hsing. In the spring of the following year, 1893, the wedding took place. Although Tseng P'u stayed at home that year, he continued to work on his bibliographic study. As mentioned before, by the summer of 1890, Tseng P'u had already collected over five hundred titles of Later Han works. He was about to organize them according to the scheme employed by Chu I-tsun (1629–1709) in his *Ching-i k'ao* (General Bibliography of the Classics), when a friend asked him if he had seen the works by Ch'ien Ta-chao (1744–1813), Hung I-sun (1773–1816), Lao Ying (nineteenth century), and Hou K'ang (1789–1837) on Later Han bibliography, which he had not.[14] His friend then persuaded him to read these works before continuing with his own. Only by supplementing the deficiencies and correcting the errors of his predecessors would he make his own study of lasting value. Tseng P'u agreed and stopped his own work temporarily.

In the autumn of 1891, Tseng P'u found the works of Hou and Ch'ien. He did not find them satisfactory; but they were helpful for supplementing his own work. He never had the opportunity to examine Hung's and Lao's works, but judging from comments about them they must have been inferior to those of Hou and Ch'ien. Very pleased with finding the worthiness of his own undertaking, Tseng P'u set to work on his compilation with greater determination than before. In the same year, 1891, he finished two chapters of critical studies on the classics and histories; and in the summer of 1892, after his disastrous Third Degree examination, he finished two more chapters of the same. In the spring of 1893, back in Ch'ang-shu, he finished one chapter of studies on literature, and another one on astronomy, medicine, religion, divination, and the other occult arts. During the spring and summer of 1894, Tseng P'u was back in Peking trying to obtain an official post. But the inertia and unresponsiveness of the bureaucracy frustrated all his attempts. He frequented the home of Weng T'ung-ho during this period, but it was to no avail. He did not obtain a post.

In the autumn, on the pretext of his grandmother Ting's eightieth birthday, Tseng P'u returned home. By winter he had finished two more chapters of studies on the annals and biographies; then in 1895, two more chapters, one on the philosophers and military tactics, and another on Buddhism and Taoism. Finally, on the fifteenth day of the sixth month, after completing a preface and other miscellaneous notes, his eleven-chapter magnum opus was completed. He began the work in 1889 and completed it six years later in 1895; during that time he sat for three examinations, married twice, was frustrated by the Sino-Japanese War, and mourned the passing of his first wife and child. These years of study laid the foundation of his knowledge of ancient and medieval Chinese literature, for he read the *Complete Works of the Ancient Period, Three Epochs, Ch'in, Han, Three Kingdoms and Six Dynasties Period* (Ch'üan shang-ku, San-tai, Ch'in, Han, San-kuo, Liu-ch'ao wen) in 741 chapters compiled by Yen K'o-chün (1762–1843). And his magnum opus marked the end of his six years of apprenticeship in classical scholarship.

These years in Peking left him with many memories of this formative period of his life. His foundation in classical literature and scholarship was laid during this period. His personal associations with eminent scholars and statesmen of the day formed many permanent impressions in his mind—these became the basis of his novel *Flower*. Many years later, his lifelong friend Chang Hung commented on Tseng P'u's literary accomplishments in this way: "The people today regard you highly as a proponent of the new literature, but I think you derive your strength from the solid foundation you have in classical literature giving you great versatility and power." [15]

CHAPTER 3

Tseng P'u and French Literature

CHINA'S defeat in the Sino-Japanese War of 1894–95 was a rude awakening to the complacent Self-strengtheners of the late Ch'ing period who had tried to modernize China by merely adopting Western technology without making any institutional changes. It was a minimal response to Westernization which began in the 1860s after the Taiping Rebellion (1850–64). After the war, memorials, essays, and poetry were written in abundance attacking officials and commanders for their misconduct of the war, lamenting the soldiers who died in battle, and begrudging the loss of territory and honor in the aftermath of the war. Even Tseng P'u's father, the mild-mannered country *literatus*, wrote an essay entitled "On the Four Just Causes for and Three Advantages of Subjugating the Japanese" [1] in which he argued forcefully for going to war against Japan for her infringements on China's vassal state Korea. Wen T'ing-shih, backed by a host of other officials, led an attack on Li Hung-Chang (1823–1901) and his subordinates for the ignoble conduct of the war and his conciliatory posture in the negotiations. In the autumn of 1895, after the conclusion of the war, the College of Foreign Languages (*T'ung-wen Kuan*) began another class in foreign languages. One of the new students in the French class was Tseng P'u.

I A Student of French at the T'ung-wen College

At the outbreak of the Sino-Japanese War in 1894 Tseng P'u was a young man of twenty-two. He had been in Peking off and on for three or four years and had frequented the home of Weng T'ung-ho who was a good friend of the family. However, even before open hostilities between China and Japan began, Tseng P'u realized how hopeless it was for a Second Degree holder with a purchased office to be heard on the issues of the day. In the fall of 1894, completely discouraged, Tseng P'u asked for leave to return to Ch'ang-shu. It was also the occasion of his grandmother Ting's eightieth birthday. On August 1, the Sino-Japanese War was officially declared.

With his back turned on the current scene, Tseng P'u enjoyed the bliss of a family reunion at T'ao-yüan in Kiangsu, while the war raged in the north. The place was serene and delightful. The name T'ao-yüan immediately calls to mind the idyllic utopia described in the poet T'ao-Ch'ien's (365–427) famous prose-poem "Peach Blossom Spring" (*T'ao-hua yüan chi*) [2] where the people have not heard of war or strife for generations. T'ao-yüan became, temporarily, Tseng P'u's refuge from the harsh realities of the outside world. The hostilities ended in March, 1895, and on April 17 the Treaty of Shimonoseki was signed. The loss of the Liaotung Peninsula and Taiwan to Japan, together with other concessions to the English, French, Russians, and Germans was heartbreaking to the patriotic soul of a loyal Chinese.

After the year's stay at T'ao-yüan, Tseng P'u could no longer shut himself off from the disturbing news outside and sit idly by on the sidelines. In consultation with his father, Tseng P'u decided to return to Peking to study French at the T'ung-wen College. This was a way for him to learn about the West, and to aid China in her attempt to modernize. Also, there was the practical consideration that the T'ung-wen College was an alternative route into the governmental bureaucracy. Training at the T'ung-wen College could lead to a position in the Tsungli Yamen, the Office of Foreign Affairs, as a translator or interpreter. With an introduction from a family friend, Mr. Yü Yu-lai, Tseng P'u enrolled in the school.

The T'ung-wen kuan, or College of Foreign Languages, was founded in 1861. [3] Although it had not always been highly regarded, it was constantly being improved by its director, W.A.P. Martin, who also taught there from 1864–1895. In its early years only poor Manchu bannermen who had no prospects elsewhere enrolled in the school. The Chinese did not enroll because it was demeaning to learn a non-Chinese "barbarian" tongue. However, beginning in the 1870s the ratio of Chinese to Manchus rose. Although in 1879 Chinese participation was lower than twenty percent, in 1888 it had risen to forty percent; in 1898, seventy-nine percent. This increase was due both to the greater importance and prestige given to Western learning, and to the fact that the college was a stepping-stone into the bureaucracy. Several of Tseng P'u's friends enrolled at the school at the same time as Tseng P'u. There was Chang Hung, P'an Sheng-nien, P'eng Ku-sun, and Weng Chiung-sun. The latter three were

Tseng P'u's new acquaintances in Peking. Ch'i Ju-shan (1877–1962), who later became a student of Peking opera, also enrolled at the school.

In the mid-1890s, however, instruction at the school had deteriorated. Martin, who had headed the college for over thirty years, resigned and was replaced by C.H. Oliver. Many of the language classes were not taught by native speakers but by Manchus or Chinese. Therefore, when Tseng P'u enrolled in the French class, he did not find the teaching satisfactory. He told us that the students were given thirty-three words a day which they were to commit to memory and recite on the following day, when another thirty-three words were introduced. At first his class was taught by a Manchu, Shih Tseng, and then by a Chinese, Te Yu-hsüan, when Shih Tseng was sent on a mission abroad.

The aim of the language program was to train high-level translators and interpreters. In the 1890s some of the students enrolled were already officials and others had passed some of the civil service examinations. The high qualification of these students, however, created other problems for the teachers. They were too proud and stubborn to study. Tseng P'u writes,

Who would have known that the special students selected for this class, who were either officials or learned scholars, were too busy and too proud to bow their heads over their desks and study like little children? Every day when they went to the class, it was like going to their offices (yamen); they would just sit for a while, drink a cup of tea, chit-chat, and go through the motions of studying to satisfy their superiors. The foreign instructors could not do a thing. They came to class, performed a solo, and then left. As time passed, they became bored with this routine and often neglected to come. The students also became irregular in their attendance. After maintaining itself for eight months, this special class came to an end.[4]

After eight months of instruction, Tseng P'u went home again. In spite of the poor teaching, he studied earnestly and learned the fundamentals of the language.

Since Tseng P'u had his mind set on entering the Tsungli Yamen, after a brief sojourn at home he returned to Peking to take a language examination in order to obtain a post as translator and/or interpreter. But he did not achieve this goal. Weng T'ung-ho recorded in his diary for September 3, 1896: "Thirty Manchus and thirty Chinese were to be awarded the position of translation secretaries from the office of the Grand Secretariat. Tseng P'u was not awarded one. Chang Hung was awarded one low on the list." After receiving the bad news, Tseng P'u went to visit Weng on the seventh; Weng recorded in his diary: "Tseng P'u came to bid me farewell. Because he did not get a post as a translation secretary, he left with a swish of his cloak." For some reason, Weng T'ung-ho did not grant Tseng P'u a post, whereas Tseng P'u's fellow student and friend Chang Hung received one. It was not that Weng did not know Tseng P'u's talents, for on May 5 of the same year, Tseng P'u presented a copy of his *Bibliographical Treatise* to Weng and the latter was amazed at his talent.[5] After this last unsuccessful attempt to enter the bureaucracy, Tseng P'u left Peking for good.

II   *Tseng P'u and Ch'en Chi-t'ung*

Three years after he left the T'ung-wen College Tseng P'u met Ch'en Chi-t'ung (1851–1907), formerly a student at the Foochow Naval School and a returned-student from France, who became his friend and private tutor in French literature. During this interim of three years Tseng P'u did not give up his study of French whereas the other students promptly forgot what they were taught. Tseng P'u retained what little he did learn and continued to study on his own. He struggled with a French reader and a dictionary. Every day he would study his reader, look up the new words in the dictionary, note them down in red, then commit them to memory. As we mentioned in Chapter 1, he did have a good memory. Finding that this method still did not give him the desired results, he hung a blackboard in a hallway which he passed frequently, and wrote on this blackboard the words he wanted to learn. Whenever he passed the hallway, or whenever he had a spare moment, he would take a glance at the blackboard. After three years of diligent study in this fashion, he bought a copy of Anatole France's *Histoire Comique* in a secondhand bookshop. It was an exciting moment—he could read it! He was filled with enthusiasm. His years of hard work finally were rewarded. After struggling though the *Histoire Comique*, he found other writings much easier. But his reading at this time was unsystematic; he read philosophy, science, literature, whatever he could lay his hands on. Until the time of his meeting with Ch'en Chi-t'ung, Tseng P'u read aimlessly.

During these three years, Tseng P'u's study was not uninterrupted. In 1896 his father died. Tseng P'u and his father were very close; their studies, especially, brought them together. His death was a great blow to Tseng P'u. After the funeral and mourning period,

Tseng P'u went to Shanghai to conclude a business venture that his father had begun. It was this mission to Shanghai that led to his association with the reformists and the meeting with Ch'en Chi-t'ung. Also during this period, Tseng P'u had his second son, Yao-chung, in the spring of 1896, and a daughter, Te, in the fourth month of 1897.

In 1898 while he was in Shanghai, Tseng P'u was invited by his friend Chiang Piao to help host a farewell party for the bold reformer T'an Ssu-t'ung (1865–1898), who was later that year to become a martyr in the aftermath of the Hundred Days Reform Movement, before his ill-fated departure for Peking.

It may be useful here to note briefly the important political event of that year, the Hundred Days Reform of 1898 (June 11–September 21). That reform effort was one example of the confrontation between the forces of change and the forces of the status quo, in which the latter won in this instance. The movement was led by the energetic, young intellectuals, K'ang Yu-wei (1858–1927), Liang Ch'i-ch'ao (1873–1929), and others, and later joined by T'an Ssu-t'ung, who was also a philosopher in his own right. Liang Ch'i-ch'ao was a year younger than Tseng P'u, and T'an Ssu-t'ung, whom Tseng P'u met, was seven years his senior. These reformers gained the ear of the Kuang-hsü Emperor, who was just twenty-seven at the time (one year older than Tseng P'u), and tried to put through a series of more than forty reform measures to revolutionize the Ch'ing governmental system. But it was too much too soon. Opposition mounted. Then on September 21, the young emperor was seized in a coup d'état led by the Empress Dowager and the reforms came to an abrupt end. Six reformers were captured and put to death, including T'an Ssu-t'ung. Tseng P'u is an example of an individual caught between similar conflicting forces. He, however, because of his background, temperament, and disillusionment with the officialdom did not join the reform movement.

At the farewell banquet for T'an, Tseng P'u was introduced to a General Ch'en Chi-t'ung, who had lived in France for a number of years and knew French literature well. They became friends immediately. After their first meeting, Tseng P'u went to visit him frequently to ask him for instruction in French literature. Soon General Ch'en became Tseng P'u's private tutor in French literature.

Ch'en Chi-t'ung had been a student at the Foochow Naval School. He went to France for the first time in 1874 with Prosper Giguel (1835–1886), the foreign director of the naval school from 1866–1874, as one of the five graduates of the school. He went a second time in 1877 as the secretary of Giguel, who accompanied twenty-six students of the school to study in France. While in Paris, Ch'en studied French, and then European and international law, possibly at L'É cole Libre des Science Politiques or the Faculté de Droite of the Université de Paris. Later he became a popular figure in Paris. Henri Cordier, the famous French sinologist, referred to him as knowing more about France than about China. Ch'en remained in France for a good number of years, where he served as Chinese military attaché in the 1880s, rising to the rank of general by 1886. He also took a French wife. His popularity in Paris was due to several works that he wrote and published in France. His works included: (1) a novel entitled *Le Roman de L'Homme Jaune*, (2) a translation of Chinese myths and folktales, *Contes Chinois*, (3) a description of Paris as seen by a Chinese, *Les Parisiens Peints par un Chinois*, (4) a work about China, *Mon Pays*, (5) the amusements of the Chinese, *Les Plaisirs en Chine*, and (6) a play, *L'Homme de la Robe Jaune*.[6] In his later years he still received royalties from his works published in France.

Ch'en Chi-t'ung, like most students who went to study abroad, was thirsty for new knowledge and read widely. Ch'en was well versed in French literature and a good teacher. When Tseng P'u came to ask him about French literature, Ch'en Chi-t'ung furnished him with an extensive reading list. According to Tseng P'u, among the Classicists, Ch'en had him read Rabelais' *Gargantua*, the poetry of Ronsard, the tragedies of Racine and Molière, *L'Art Poétique* of Boileau, the *Pensées* of Pascal, and the essays of Montaigne. Among the Romanticists, Tseng P'u, under Ch'en's direction, read Rousseau's essays, the novels of Victor Hugo, the poetry of Vigny, the plays of Dumas père, and the history of Michelet. Among the Naturalist writers, he read the novels of Flaubert, Zola, and Maupassant, the poetry of Leconte de Lisle, the plays of Dumas *fils*, and the criticism of Taine. And among the moderns he read the *La Littérature et l'Epoque: Histoire de la Littérature Française de 1885 à nos Jours* by Florian Parmentier, and the works of Alphonse Daudet, Anatole France, and Pierre Loti. This was not all. Ch'en also introduced Tseng P'u to Italian, Spanish, English, and German works which had been translated into French. Thanks to Ch'en's introduction, Tseng P'u made contact with several bookstores in France. In the next three to four years he was able to buy and study many other works in French literature and philosophy.

Ch'en Chi-t'ung not only taught Tseng P'u French literature, but he also told him about the status of Chinese literature in Europe, particularly in France. Ch'en's message was that Chinese literature was not highly regarded by Westerners generally, but by the exceptional few: Voltaire had criticized Chinese poetry for its lack of development, and Anatole France had criticized Chinese literature for being vulgar and crude. Ch'en believed that the reason for this was, first, that the Chinese had not made any effort to introduce their literature properly to the West, and second, that the Chinese had put their efforts and emphasis on literary genres that were not popular in the West. Therefore, a misconception had arisen about Chinese literature. Ch'en's solution for putting an end to this misconception was, on the one hand, to translate Chinese literature into various Western languages, and on the other to translate Western literature into Chinese. In order for China to enter the arena of world literature, she must change her literary practices.

Ch'en's message left a lasting impression on Tseng P'u; he was to write about it almost thirty years later in a long letter to Hu Shih in 1928. These remarks are still timely today:

To survive in these times, we must not only study science, but also literature. In the field of literature, we must not be haughty and boastful, consider ourselves to be the only nation with a literary heritage, and care nothing about the developments of other peoples. If we ignore others, then when it comes time to reckon the literatures of the world, we will not be recognized. We will be even lagging behind the Japanese.

Among the foreign countries, I have been in France the longest, and I have frequently come in contact with her people. Often I have heard them express their sentiments about China, and they make me jump up and down with anger. Only a few experts in the field are fair-minded, like Abel Remusat, who is a specialist on Chinese literature and wrote a book on the Chinese language and literature, and M. Guillaume Pauthier, who reveres Chinese philosophy. His translations include the *Analects* of Confucius, the *Mencius*, the *Classic of Poetry*, and *Lao Tzu*. He believes that Confucius and Mencius were moralists and political philosophers, and that the *Lao Tzu* is a work of supreme rationalism.

Then there are Guillard d'Arcy, who has translated a number of Chinese myths and entitled his work *Contes Chinois*; Stanislas Julien, who has done translations of two Chinese tales, *Les Deux Jeune Filles Lettres*, and *Les Deux Cousines*; and P. d'Entre-Colles, who has translated a Chinese story which he entitled *Histoire de la Dame à L'Éventail Blanc*. The translations of Chinese literature were done half in jest and half in appreciation. As for the attitude of others, if it were not one of belittling, then it was one of disgust. Even Voltaire, the great admirer of Chinese civilization, in a letter to the Duc de

Richelieu with which he prefaced his play *L'Orphelin de la Chine* (based on
an earlier translation of a Chinese play by Joseph Prémare), praised the
Chinese for having discovered the art of poetic drama three thousand years
ago, . . . but condemned us for making such slow progress since then, and
for retaining the same attitudes of three thousand years ago. As for the
modern literary giant Anatole France, he berates us without restraint. In
criticizing our literature, he says that superficially our prose and poetry
appear dignified and refined, but underneath they express the thoughts of a
despicable people. In criticizing our myths and legends, he says that most of
them leave the reader unsatisfied because they are crude and unconvincing.
The descriptions of tragic events seem merely theatrical. In a word, Chinese
literature is unbearably bad. This type of criticism is openly printed in the
newspapers.

I feel that we have reached this state of affairs for two reasons: first, we do
not pay attention to publicizing our works. Few of our works are translated
into a Western language, and those which have been translated are either
inferior works in themselves or are poorly translated, thus hindering better
understanding. Second, the area of our literary concern differs from that of
the Westerners. For us, poetry, belles-lettres, and a few other genres are the
literary forms par excellence. But the Westerners put great emphasis on
novels and plays, which we look down upon. Therefore, the misunder-
standing.

Now we must not be content to confine ourselves to learning about the
literature of only one nation. We must learn about the literature of the world.
And since we want to become part of the worldwide literary scene, we must
remove these obstacles; we must encourage not only large-scale translations
of our great works of literature into Western languages, but also translate
great works of Western literature into Chinese. To avoid further misunder-
standing, we must alter our accustomed literary practices. We must abandon
our prejudices and change our literary forms to conform with those of the
West. Most important for accomplishing these goals is to read as much
Western literature as possible.[7]

It must have been painful to an ardent student of Chinese literature
like Tseng P'u to hear that the time-honored literature of his country
was held in such low esteem in the West. For instance, Anatole
France wrote this comment concerning some of Ch'en Chi-t'ung's
translations: "As for romances, I, like the rest of the world, had read
the short stories translated at various times by Abel Remusat, Guillard d'Arcy, Stanislas Julien, and other scholars whose names I do not
recollect. . . . There remain in my head, after reading these stories,
a mixture of prose and verse, the impression of a people abominably
ferocious, but extremely polite. The Chinese tales recently published
by General Ch'en Chi-t'ung appear to me to be much more artless

than any previous translations of this nature; they are little tales
analogous to our stories of Old Mother Goose, full of dragons, vam-
pires, little foxes, flower-like women and porcelain gods. Here we
have the popular style, and may learn the tales, told by nurses in the
lamplight to the little yellow children of the Celestial Empire. . . .
The twenty-five tales collected and translated by General Ch'en
Chi-t'ung suffice to show that the Chinese have no hopes beyond this
world, and have no conception of a divine ideal. Their moral ideas,
like their paintings, are lacking in perspective and horizon. . . ." [8]

Tseng P'u took Ch'en Chi-t'ung's advice to heart; for the next three
or four years he read voraciously and often continuously through the
night without rest, in order "to read as much Western literature as
possible." Although spiritually he was fulfilled, the immediate physical consequence of his industriousness was a serious illness which
lasted for three years and damaged his basic constitution. He was
bedridden off and on for the years from 1900 to 1903, during which
time his wife patiently nursed him back to health. Tseng P'u's diligence was also to bring him an unexpected feeling of isolation and
loneliness: alienation.

III   Disappointment with Lin Shu and Alienation

French was Tseng P'u's window on the outside world, but at the
same time, it was the cause of his alienation from his own culture and
society. With his newly acquired knowledge of French literature and
philosophy, Tseng P'u was anxious to exchange ideas with those
around him; but he found that no one shared his interests. Most of his
contemporaries were interested only in the Western social or natural
sciences; few if any were interested in Western literature. Tseng P'u
felt isolated and alone. He wrote:

. . . at the time everybody was enthusiastically worshipping the Westerners, their science and technology, their sturdy ships and fierce cannons.
Sometimes when I talked about Western poetry, everyone stared with
astonishment. How could the crabbing, wormlike script of the Westerners
express anything beautiful! They thought I was telling them fairytales! Sometimes when I told them about the prestige that fiction and drama enjoyed in
Western society, they thought that it was because the cultural level of the
Westerners was low; having nothing else to boast about, they made much of
fiction and drama. When I spoke about the social thought of Saint-Simon and
Fourier, they thought that I was a rebel. When I talked about Nietzsche's
idea of *Übermensch*, they thought I was talking heresy. [9]

At the turn of the century most Chinese were interested only in the physical sciences, technology, and languages. The emphasis was on practical knowledge. The subjects taught in the early government schools, such as the T'ung-wen College, Foochow Naval School, and the Kiangnan Arsenal, were physics, chemistry, mathematics, astronomy, languages, and other technical subjects. No place was given to the humanities. When the students were sent abroad to study, they continued with their study of technical subjects. Only a few studied international law and other social science subjects. A glance at the translations made during this period (1850 to 1904) substantiates this practical tendency. Among the four large categories of learning (the social sciences, natural sciences, applied sciences, and the humanities), the social sciences rank first with 367 translations, the applied sciences rank second with 286, with the natural sciences a close third with 281, and finally the humanities with only eighty-six translations.[10] China's interest in Western literature began in earnest only with Lin Shu's translation of *La Dame aux Camèlias* by Alexandre Dumas *fils* in 1895, which was one of the most popular translated works in China.

Tseng P'u was unusual in that he had learned a foreign language on his own without having gone abroad, and in that he read only those works that were of interest to him. If he had gone abroad to study, he probably would have been compelled to study natural sciences and other technical subjects. As it was, he read much literature, but he found no one in his circle of friends who was interested in Western literature and could discuss these matters with him. He wrote:

> Because I was infatuated with what was said by Ch'en Chi-t'ung, not only did I become seriously ill, but for many years I felt the bitterness of isolation. A man's social nature makes him anxious to communicate with his fellow beings about his experiences; only then can he have fulfillment. But after having painstakingly studied many books and acquired new knowledge, I found that I could only imitate Li Po's "drinking in solitude with only the moon and my shadow as companions." I had only myself to talk with; I could not find anyone else who shared my interests.[11]

Unable to find companionship among those around him, Tseng P'u turned to Lin Shu (1852–1924) whose translations of Western literature began appearing in large numbers about this time.

At first there was mutual admiration between the two men who knew each other only by their works. Of course, Lin Shu was the more famous of the two men. Lin Shu later became the most prolific

translator of Western fiction in modern China. His translation of
Dumas *fils*' *La Dame aux Camèlias* brought him immediate fame. It is
interesting to note that Lin came in contact with Western literature
accidentally when a friend brought him a copy of Dumas' novel. The
story appealed to him so much that he became addicted to Western
fiction. In his lifetime he translated more than 180 Western works.
Ironically, he did not read any foreign languages, and his translations
had to be done through an interpreter. But this did not hinder his
progress. Lin became one of the most outstanding literary figures in
modern Chinese literature—even if anachronistic, because he translated these works of fiction into *ku-wen* or the literary language rather
than the colloquial language.

In the preface to his translation of Rider Haggard's *Beatrice* in
1906,[12] Lin Shu wrote that he had read Tseng P'u's novel *A Flower in
an Ocean of Sin* with delight. He agreed wholeheartedly with the
author's criticism of the literati-aristocracy in Peking, and noted that
Flower was not truly a work of fiction, but a work that aroused the
heroic valor of the Chinese people. Since *Flower* was published
under the *nom de plume* of Tung-ya-ping-fu (The Sick Man of East
Asia) and Ai-tzu-yu-che (The Lover of Freedom), Lin Shu lamented
the fact that he did not know who the actual authors were. By 1908,
however, Lin Shu had learned that Tung-ya ping-fu was Tseng P'u. In
the preface to his translation of Dickens' *Oliver Twist*,[13] he expressed
his sadness at the passing of the famous late Ch'ing writer Li Po-yüan
(1867–1906), but was encouraged that men like Tseng P'u and Liu E
(1857–1909) were still writing, who like Charles Dickens could point
out the evils of society to the officials and the public.

Tseng P'u, of course, knew Lin Shu from reading his translations.
He was especially impressed with the speed of Lin Shu's translations.
He noted that Lin's translations of Sir Walter Scott's long novels, *The
Talisman* and *The Betrothed*, appeared only six months apart. Tseng
P'u read these works with enthusiasm and thought that from then on
he had someone with whom he could talk. Probably in 1907, Tseng
P'u made a trip to Peking to visit Lin Shu. To his disappointment
Tseng P'u found that Lin Shu did not know any foreign languages and
did not understand the history and development of Western literature. He was completely dependent on his collaborators for materials
to be translated. Tseng P'u explained to him the various schools and
trends of writing in European literature and tried to persuade him to
be more systematic in his choice of works, otherwise he would be
merely adding to his already extensive list of translations, rather than

influencing the development of Chinese literature. Finally, Tseng P'u made two suggestions: first, that Lin Shu use the vernacular rather than the literary language so that his translations would reach a wider audience and preserve more of the spirit of the original; second, he advised Lin Shu to be more selective and systematic in his choice of literary works. But Lin Shu was not receptive to these suggestions. Tseng P'u left with the impression that Lin Shu was confused, opinionated, and at times displayed a willful arrogance. His inability to communicate with Lin Shu caused him to withdraw deeper into isolation. He wrote, "after I found that Lin Shu could not fulfill my hopes and expectations, I did not wish to discuss literature again with anyone. . . ." [14]

IV   *The Origins of Tseng P'u's Romanticism*

Although Tseng P'u was not able to find anyone with whom he could discuss French literature, he did not cease to read it nor did he lose interest in literature as a whole. He continued with his study of French, writing about various French authors and translating their works.

While he abandoned his literary career and left the literary field from 1908 to 1926 to play an active part in the politics of Kiangsu province, he continued his study of literature and published a work now and then. In 1913 his translation of Victor Hugo's *Quatre-vingt Treize* was published, and in 1916 his translation of Hugo's play *Lucrèce Borgia*. While his son Yao-chung was studying medicine in Europe in 1919, Tseng P'u had him purchase books so that he could write a history of French literature.

When Tseng P'u published *Lu Nan-tzu: Lien* (Love) in 1927, he had, by then, completed his formulation of a romantic hero in the Chinese context. It was his synthesis of the ideals of French Romanticism with the Chinese "romantic" hero epitomized by Chia Pao-yu of *The Dream of the Red Chamber*. Tseng P'u arrived at this formulation by combining his study and translation of four French writers— Balzac, Molière, Zola, and Victor Hugo—with the Chinese literary tradition. These four authors, then, were the main source of Tseng P'u's romanticism.

Tseng P'u was not only interested in the literary works of these writers, as such, but also in their lives. He was fascinated by the French way of life: the excitement of the French salons, and the romantic, spontaneous French nature. In an essay entitled "The

Story of Balzac's Marriage," Tseng P'u wrote: "Reading about the loves of George Sand and Alfred de Musset stimulated me to gather materials on the love-life and marriage of famous writers." The reasoning was that a talented writer was usually unconventional in his behavior. He felt that their every act, whether it be done out of frivolity, loneliness, madness, or desperation, always contained elements of poetry and imagination. And their experiences were always related to their works. Therefore, if one understood their lives, he would have a clearer understanding of their works.[15] Tseng P'u did not intend to idealize the artists or weep over their sorrows.

In the case of Honoré de Balzac, aside from his works, Tseng P'u was interested in the seventeen-year-long romance between Balzac and the Polish Countess Eveline Hanska. The question that intrigued Tseng P'u was whether or not Balzac was really happy after he was finally married. The answer, he concluded, was no. He understood Balzac as a man full of illusions; Balzac had illusions of becoming a great politician, of becoming a millionaire, and his long romance with Eveline Hanska was no exception. Tseng P'u did not think that Mme Hanska was worthy of Balzac, for she did not really understand him. The fact that she sold all his papers, manuscripts, and everything else indicated that she did not really love him. Tseng P'u concluded that we should feel sorry that Balzac was under the illusion that his dreams of acquiring wealth and honor, of finding true love were fulfilled by marrying the Polish countess. In fact, he died in loneliness and despair. Five months after his marriage, he paid for his decision with his life.

In 1927 Tseng P'u translated Molière's comedy *L'École des Femmes* and wrote about the four women in Molière's life: Madeleine Béjart, Catherine de Brie, Mlle du Parc, and Armande Béjart who became his wife. Tseng P'u was not unaware of the autobiographical significance of the play. Molière, at the age of forty, married the twenty-year-old Armande Béjart, who was suspected of being his own daughter and was carrying on an affair with another man. Tseng P'u must have noticed the parallel between Arnolphe and his ward Agnes in the play with Molière and his young wife Armande.

Madeleine Béjart, four years older than Molière, was a very capable woman and a good partner for Molière in the theater. Mlle du Parc was a fiery beauty and an excellent actress and singer who rejected Molière's advances. In disappointment he turned to Catherine de Brie, who was a much more gentle person, and they remained lovers and friends for the rest of their lives. All four of these women were members of Molière's theatrical troupe, L'Illustre Théâtre. Tseng P'u's observation was:

These four women in Molière's life brought him sorrow and pain, but also joy and happiness. The two who were kind to him were Madeleine Béjart and Catherine de Brie; the two that caused him pain were Mlle du Parc and Armande Béjart. For better or for worse, these were the forces that shaped his development. The tranquility of blissful love gave him the opportunity to observe life and to write satire; the pains of jealousy and troubled love, embodying tones of distress, enabled his works to reveal the deeper meanings of life. Therefore, today when we read the comedies of Molière, everywhere we feel the joy and sadness of his personal experience. The heroines in his plays are, in part, embodiments of these four women. Since each of the characters speaks as a person in real life, no wonder Molière's comedies are so moving.[16]

In April, 1928, Tseng P'u's translations of Émile Zola's two novellas *Nantas* and *Madame Neigeon* were published. Although these stories predate Zola's grand scheme of the Rougon-Macquart cycle, they also deal with the struggles of individuals against the environment in their upward climb in society. The first tale tells of Nantas, a young man from a working family, a nobody, who works his way up to become finance minister in the Second Empire through a chance and loveless marriage to Mlle Flavie, the daughter of the powerful Baron Danvilliers. However, as Nantas becomes more and more successful, he becomes more and more in love with his wife, who is cool and aloof. Heartbroken, Nantas, on the eve of his greatest financial triumph, prepares to commit suicide. Just as he raises the revolver to his head, Mlle Flavie rushes into the room and saves him by expressing her genuine love and admiration for him: "I love you, for you are truly strong."

Madame Neigeon is a tale about the wiles and coquetries of Parisian high society women who use their beauty to achieve their own ends. An inexperienced young man from the country becomes the victim of the charming, dark-haired Madame Neigeon, who needs to get votes for her husband in an election for General Councillor. After securing his vote, Mme Neigeon abruptly rejects the advances of the young man with an unexpected strong rebuke. Tseng P'u comments:

Nantas can be said to express the greatness of "human energy" and the hardships of man's struggle against the environment. After reading the story,

the pages seem to glow with flames. *Madame Neigeon* is different. If we use
the analogy of the five flavors, then *Nantas* is like the hotness of peppers, and
Madame Neigeon the sourness of vinegar, because in the latter, the author
uses the technique of satire to expose the baseness of political intrigue.[17]

Victor Hugo and his writings, particularly his plays, were the single
greatest influence on Tseng P'u in his later literary career. He translated four of Hugo's plays: *Hernani, Ruy Blas, Lucrèce Borgia,* and
Angelo; one novel, *Quatre-vingt Treize*; and *La Esmeralda,* the
operatic version of the novel *Notre-Dame-de-Paris*. What was it that
drew Tseng P'u to Hugo? It may have been Hugo's many-sidedness,
his dynamic personality, his life of action, and his career as a writer.

Victor Hugo was born on February 26, 1802, and died on May 12,
1885, his long life spanning almost the whole of the nineteenth
century. He participated fully in the political, social, and literary
activities of his time; he tried his hand at all the various genres of
literary writing—with varying degrees of success. As a writer, he may
be looked upon from these three aspects: as dramatist, novelist, and
lyric poet. From an early age Hugo displayed a penchant for the
"grandiose, the tremendous, and the horrific" and was attracted to
the melodramatic, the sensational, and the bizarre.[18] Hugo was not
only a literary figure, but also a political personality, and later became
a national hero. He had a powerful personality which exuded from all
his works and actions. In his study of French literature Geoffrey
Brereton wrote that Victor Hugo's "triumphant personality and
work, full of extravagant colors, mark the influx of French Romanticism at its most confident and maintained themselves long after the
tide would appear to have ebbed." [19]

Tseng P'u's translation of *Quatre-vingt Treize* was published in
1913. This was the last of Hugo's grand, lyrical novels which include
Notre-Dame-de-Paris (1831), *Les Misérables* (1862), *Les Travailleurs
de la Mer* (1866), and *L'Homme qui Rit* (1869). The events of *Quatre-
vingt Treize* took place in 1793, the year in which Europe was
attacking France. It was the year of the French civil war. On a smaller
scale, this civil war is being waged between the members of an
aristocratic family, Marquis de Lantenac, an old man in his eighties,
and his grand-nephew Vicomte de Gauvain, a young man in his
prime. The dramatic intensity of the novel is brought to a high point
by the four pathetic victims of the war, an innocent war widow and
her three young children. It is the suffering of these unfortunate
victims that brings out the basic human qualities in these men who

have been hunting each other down like wild beasts. Near the end of the novel, as the marquis is about to escape capture, he hears the voice of the wretched mother (the war widow) crying out for her children. He stops: "The mother's shriek had stirred within him the dregs of human pity,—the deposit of universal life which exists in every soul, even the most cruel." Old Lantenac saves the children and as a result is captured. It must have been the interplay between toughness and tenderness, the young and the old, that attracted Tseng P'u.

Lucrèce Borgia was the next work that Tseng P'u translated into Chinese. The central idea of *Lucrèce Borgia* is maternal love, an important concept in the Romantic imagination. Hugo uses this all-powerful, purifying idea of love, which can transform a moral monster into an object of love and pity, to evoke our deepest emotions. He makes this point perfectly clear in the preface to the play:

What is the inmost thought concealed beneath the three or four concentric thickness of bark in *Lucrèce Borgia*? Take the most hideous, the most repulsive, the most complete moral deformity, place it where it is best set off. In the heart of a woman, with all the conditions of physical beauty and royal grandeur which give prominence to crime; and now mingle with all this moral deformity a pure sentiment, the purest that woman can experience—the maternal sentiment; in the monster put a mother, and the monster will interest, and the monster will call forth tears, and this creature that caused fear will cause pity, and this deformed soul will become almost beautiful in your eyes; thus maternity purifying moral deformity, that is Lucrèce Borgia.[20]

Like the romantic audience of Hugo's time, Tseng P'u was attracted to the antithesis between moral depravity and the pure goodness of maternal love, a union of the grotesque and the sublime. Tseng P'u notes in his translation:

The intrigues and assassinations of the Borgia family were the most shocking and licentious in all Italian history. Lucrèce is a master of this kind of intrigue; at the same time she is a woman and a mother. How can one not marvel at the skill of Hugo who invested the purest maternal love in the bosom of such a woman! [21]

Tseng P'u's translation first appeared in 1916, and it was later reprinted in 1927.

Tseng P'u's translation of *Hernani* was published in 1927. The plot of the play centers around the ultimate romantic hero, Hernani, an outlawed bandit, brought up close to nature, who had been destined to be an aristocratic lord. Hernani is motivated by the dominant passion of avenging his father who was killed by the father of the present king, Don Carlos. But he fails and dies because of a gentleman's promise which he made to Don Gomez. If Hernani is the victim of the rigid, inflexible, and aristocratic code of honor, then Doña Sol, Hernani's beloved, is the impersonation of spontaneity, purity, and goodness. And she dies with him. The historic significance of the play which ushered in the Romantic era in France was not lost on Tseng P'u either. He comments:

This bold work represents the Romantic movement breaking down the barriers of Classicism. The heroine of the play spurns the love of her king and a noble to love an outlawed bandit. The unexpected twists and turns of the plot made the play an ultimate expression of Romanticism.[22]

Ruy Blas, the next play Tseng P'u translated, is a romantic tragedy in five acts. The play centers around a lackey, Ruy Blas, with the heart of a king, who falls in love with the Queen, Doña Maria de Neubourg. To the romantic imagination love can bridge all gaps and transcend all obstacles so that even someone in the lowest form of servitude, that of an entirely selfless lackey, can become the lover of the queen if his love is genuine. The story is set in the last years of the seventeenth century, when the Spanish empire is on the decline and its ministers work only for their own interests. Tseng P'u was struck by the similarities between the political chaos of early Republican China and the chaos of seventeenth-century Spain. Tseng P'u comments:

. . . at the time I was serving in Nanking. . . . I often felt that the unrestrained greed of those in power, and the ruthlessness of the militarists were in no small measure like the ministers and officials under the reign of Charles II of Spain. Inspired by the idea, I read the pages of *Ruy Blas* over and over again, and felt that Hugo's every sentence expressed exactly what I wanted to say.[23]

La Esmeralda, the operatic version of the novel *Notre-Dame-de-Paris*, was the next work that Tseng P'u translated. Quasimodo, the gargoyle-like monster who tolls the bells of Notre-Dame, and Esmeralda, the pure gypsy girl, are classic examples of "the fruitful union of the grotesque and the sublime." [24] And Hugo fully exploited the rich potential of the grotesque when it is cast alongside the sublime. It should be noted that Tseng P'u translated this work into colloquial

Chinese verse with meter and rhyme, an innovative experiment in modern Chinese poetry.

Angelo is the last of Hugo's plays that Tseng P'u translated into Chinese. It is a circular love-tragedy set in mid-sixteenth-century Padua. The tragic heroine, Tisbe, is fated to die for Catarina, her rival in love, because the latter, as a young girl, had once saved the life of Tisbe's mother. Her sense of honor and gratefulness drives Tisbe, the lowly actress-courtesan, to perform the supreme act of self-sacrifice, in order that her beloved Rodolfo and Catarina may live. Tseng P'u was most moved by this work; he described it as being the most exciting and emotionally turbulent of Hugo's plays and thought it to be his greatest dramatic achievement.

Although Hugo's plays were extremely popular during the period of the French Romantic theater from the 1830s to the 1840s, after that they have not been highly regarded critically. The plots of his plays were unnecessarily long, complicated, and contrived; the dramatic action depended on numerous devices of the Romantic theater, such as secret doors, rare poisons, sleeping potions, daggers, mysterious keys, etc. Most of Hugo's characters are two-dimensional, and they appear to be deliberately used to demonstrate Hugo's aesthetic principles. A critical evaluation of Hugo's plays, however, does not concern us here. We are only interested in finding out how these works influenced Tseng P'u and his later work *Lu Nan-tzu*.

Molière and Balzac attracted Tseng P'u partly because of the many romances in their personal lives. Tseng P'u must have empathized with them in their joy and elation, sorrow and bitterness, which he had also experienced in his own life. Tseng P'u found that he was not alone in his disappointments in love: Balzac's lifelong romance ended in sadness; Molière's marriage with his young wife was scandalous. These true-to-life incidents must have encouraged Tseng P'u to write about his own experiences. Zola introduced most poignantly the conflict between the individual and his environment. The environment, whether it be emotional, physical, social, or biological, is always pitted against the individual. It is a continuous struggle from which one cannot escape. This view of an endless struggle in which the individual must be able to face defeat and live on is important to Tseng P'u. Victor Hugo and French Romanticism undoubtedly exerted the greatest influence on Tseng P'u; the passionate, emotion-driven, hypersensitive, romantic hero, the many twists and turns of the plot, the artificial devices and missing links are clearly in evidence in *Lu Nan-tzu*.

V   *Lu Nan-tzu*

In his creation of the youthful romantic hero Lu Nan-tzu, Tseng P'u was actually rebelling against the unrestrained expression of the self as found in the early writings of the Creation Society, as represented by Kuo Mo-jo (1892–1978), Yü Ta-fu (1896–1945), and others.[25] He objected to those modern Chinese writers who depicted their heroes as Werthers or Jean-Christophes. He remarked: "The heroes commit suicide and fight duels at the slightest provocation. The young men in their despair are like Werthers, and in their heroic struggles are like Jean-Christophes. Actually, the Chinese are habitually more restrained and, by nature, more harmonious." [26]

What was the impact of these novels—whose heroes Tseng P'u criticized—on the Chinese readers of the time? Goethe's *The Sorrows of Young Werther* was translated by Kuo Mo-jo in 1921 and he noted these characteristics about the young hero and its author: (1) his emotionalism, (2) his pantheism, (3) his praise of nature, (4) his admiration of the primitive life, and (5) his respect for children.[27] The translation met with a most dramatic reception. Chinese youths wrote love letters, suicide notes, carried worn-out copies of *Werther*, and named themselves after Werther and Charlotte. The appeal of Werther to the Chinese audience was due to the intensity of his emotions, his sensitivity, his sentimentality, and the autobiographical and confessional style of the book. It was a far cry from the impersonal, objective, and terse style of classical Chinese literature. The autobiographical style tore down the barrier between the author and his reader.

Romain Rolland's *Jean-Christophe* was translated by Ching Yin-yü in 1926. The response to *Jean-Christophe* was again overwhelming. In contrast to Werther, it was Jean-Christophe's dynamism and larger-than-life heroic proportions that appealed to Chinese readers. Furthermore, Jean-Christophe had the toughness and elemental power to overcome adversity and to withstand suffering. He was above all a robust fighter, as contrasted with Werther who was a bookish, melancholy dreamer. Tseng P'u rejected both of these heroes in favor of a Chinese romantic hero who embodied the Chinese cultural characteristics of "harmony and restraint." In the late 1920s, Tseng P'u was apparently in sympathy with a group of writers who advocated the expression of the "national [spirit]" in literature (*min-tsu chu-i wen-i*).[28]

Although, both in terms of its virtues and defects, Tseng P'u's *Lu*

Nan-tzu bears a strong resemblance to such archetypal Romantic novels as Goethe's *The Sufferings of Young Werther*, or Chateaubriand's *René*, it is based on a fundamentally different moral system. (For a synopsis of the story, see Chapter 1, Section IV.) The hero, Lu Nan-tzu, is a young man of seventeen who is passionately in love with his cousin; but the social custom does not permit them to marry. Faced with this dilemma, the young hero contemplates suicide many times. But he ultimately decides against it because of moral obligations to his family and society. It was within these social constraints that Tseng P'u expressed the moral and emotional turmoil of the young man, at the same time kept the actions of the hero in conformity with Chinese "restraint" and "harmony." However, the emotional excesses, the intensive self-analysis, of *Lu Nan-tzu* equal the most extreme of its genre.

Love, central to any Romanticist writing, was the motivating force of *Lu Nan-tzu*. To Tseng P'u, love was like a mysterious, subterranean reservoir of restless energy ready to burst out into the open at any time. He wrote:

Man's life is like a boundless sea; love is like the waves of the sea. A boat drifts on the sea, bobs up and down, goes with or against the current, at times peaceful and tranquil, at times violent and precarious; it is not controlled by the oars or rudder of the boat, but by the waves. In the same way, man's behavior in the world, as long as he is not an unfeeling piece of wood or stone, although it appears to be under the influence of his mind, is actually controlled by the forces of love. Love can make you rise up, advance, seek adventure, and struggle; it can make you accomplish anything you want. Love can also make you lose all ambition, make you mad, tyrannical, and base; it can destroy everything you have accomplished.

From the very beginning of history, all the accomplishments of man, whether beautiful or ugly, recorded in writing or sung orally . . . speaking frankly, are nothing but crystallizations that have been spewed forth from the mouth of the blazing volcano of love. Nothing in life is sacred except love; there is no other destiny in life but love; and there is no purpose in life except to love.[29]

Besides love, purity, innocence, self-deprecation, melancholy, despair, rebellion, all play an important part in *Lu Nan-tzu*. Blood letters, suicides, crucial last-minute revelations add dramatic intensity to the story. The unabashed sentimentality of the novel is best exemplified by the long letter, reminiscent of Werther's last letter to Charlotte, that Lu Nan-tzu writes to Ch'i Wan-chung. This letter not only explains the moral conflict in Lu Nan-tzu between physical and spiritual love, but it is also Tseng P'u's own "confession" of guilt and longing for forgiveness.

Ever-beloved Wan,

Today, after a separation of more than a year, I finally have the opportunity to write to you. Alas! Sadness! I pick up my pen and the opening—the very opening makes me hesitate. Can I still call you mine? I am unworthy! I am unworthy! I am used to calling you mine, but now it is no longer true. Now, I am not yours, and you are not mine. This is a fact. But that is not important; since "who belongs to whom" is itself a question that is based on selfishness and not on love. Only true love can transcend selfishness and be everlasting. Will you permit me to call you "Ever-beloved Wan"?

. . . Wan, I am very sorry. I have actually committed an unforgivable sin. But what can I do? I can make only a frank confession. A confession is useless, but however useless, I must make it. Wan, please listen. Accept it as the last plea of a criminal, his confession before death.

Our talk under the eaves that morning last year, after the snow had stopped, was the last page in the story of our love. From then on I was engulfed in a whirlwind of misfortune. Immediately following our meeting I mourned for Hsiao-hsiung, who committed suicide by swallowing opium; then I was warned by your father not to set foot in your house again. Since seeing you was out of the question, of course, I turned quickly to asking for your hand. Then, who would have known that Aunt Wen, our steadfast supporter, had had a change of heart and was no longer on our side. My father and mother, at my constant urging, sent various people to talk to your father. But he remained adamant to the end. I remember the last time when Wang Lu-t'ing conveyed the message, your father upbraided me for being a playboy, said that I would never amount to anything, and that certainly he would not permit his delicate, flower-like daughter to be tossed into manure. Oh, Wan, you are the flower and I am the manure! These ugly words are an insult to me, but a compliment to you. You may deny them, but I should accept them. Well, what can I say? The debt that we owe our parents is boundless. Because my parents love me, they will do everything for me; and because your parents love you, they will do everything to protect you—even at the risk of offending their relatives and friends.

Ever-beloved Wan, the pain that cannot be blamed on anyone else is the worst kind. I became dejected and aimless. Didn't you ever want to end your suffering by suicide? Of course, I did. I thought of suicide every day, but I couldn't do it. Truthfully, I did not have the courage to do it, nor the proper circumstances. If Hsiao-hsiung had not suffered a ruthless beating, he would not have made the decision either. I often wished that I had been ruthlessly beaten, but I did not.

The letter continues to describe the marriage of two cousins, who then left the family, the death of his dear uncle, and the sympathetic suicide of his concubine. Because of these tragedies one following upon the other, Lu Nan-tzu states that he could not bring further sorrows to the family by committing suicide. Instead he swears to remain faithful to his cousin forever by never marrying. But this becomes impossible because of obligations to his parents: he must have a son to continue the family line.

Ah! Wan, imprisoned as I am, the only son under the ancestor's shadow and knowing that not to continue the family line is to violate the most sacred of teachings, how is it possible for me to remain faithful to you forever? On the other hand, if I were to remain faithful to you, can you disregard the love and concern of your parents . . . and announce publicly that you do not intend to marry for the rest of your life? . . . In fact, several times I did reject marriage proposals and suffered reprimands from my father. Then, I was shaken by some rumors . . . For no good reason I began to blame you and hate you; and even believed that you had really forgotten me. My love for you vanished; and my resolve to remain faithful forever dissolved. Finally, when my father raised the question of marriage with the T'angs, I consented in a state of confusion and allowed them to arrange everything.

Wan, if it had not been for the fact that I saw you today with my own eyes, how could I have known your true feelings? You have not forgotten me; it is I who have abandoned you! Otherwise, how could I have consented to have others arrange my marriage? . . .

Alas! Ever-beloved Wan! That's the way it is. What good is this admission of guilt? Since it cannot absolve me from blame, nor can it lessen the pains of my conscience. . . . It is not necessary for me to speak or write, but why do I keep on chattering and writing? Why? Let me tell you without holding anything back. Love is not the fulfillment of man's dreams! . . . You feel in your heart that if only fate had been kind, then our dreams would have come true, and we would have married and lived happily ever after. Oh, Wan! You are so foolish! In this world, love does not have permanence; there may be exceptions or accidents, but . . .

If the circumstances were changed and we were married without the slightest interference, then we would have momentary happiness, sweetness, and fulfillment. But I cannot say with confidence that our love would last, that we would not slowly drift apart, and that's all. Perhaps, we would break apart like two halves of an empty shell. I am not exaggerating. You should know that love is like a bird that should not be caged since soaring about is its true nature. . . . I have come to understand fully the nature of love. I believe that death is the only way to preserve the eternity of love; separation is the prolongation of love; but marriage is the end of love. Wan, please do not see our past as a misfortune. Since both of us are indebted to our parents, and since we do not have the courage to commit suicide like Hsiao-hsiung and Yün-feng who have preserved their love forever, then let us live on peacefully and quietly in our disappointment.

Ever-beloved Wan! Good-bye! I have finished saying what I want to say. Only one more thing, please let us not forget each other.[30]

This long letter, which contains passages of most unabashed sentimentality and tortuous self-analysis, illustrates Tseng P'u's romanticism. It is a combination of idealistic romanticism and down-to-earth practicality. The hero undergoes ruthless self-criticism. He contemplates suicide many times, but finds that he does not have the strength to carry it through. He wants to remain faithful to his beloved by renouncing marriage, but has to submit to demands of the family. Furthermore, marriage, he rationalizes, is not a guarantee of the permanence of love. In the world of the hero, true love is as elusive as trying to catch a pair of white doves with one's bare hands—the image which Tseng P'u uses at the beginning of his novel. The unattainability of their goal of marriage may be, paradoxically, the only way in which their true love can be preserved. True love "is like a bird which should not be caged since soaring about is its nature."

In European Romanticism the romantic hero is a rebel against society; he overflows with an abundance of good will and purity, and in his selfless devotion to his ideal he becomes an outcast from society. This fundamental ambivalence which he feels between himself and the outside world—his "romantic agony"—finally drives him to self-destruction.[31] Another aspect of his nature is his hypersensitivity; he lives by the stimulation of his senses. But at the same time, he is painfully self-conscious and must examine his conduct against the prevalent moral conventions or its hypocrisies. His preoccupations bring him suffering and confine him to the inner realm of his feelings and sensibilities.

The traditional Chinese romantic hero, as epitomized by Chia Pao-yü in the famous eighteenth-century Chinese novel *The Dream of the Red Chamber*, bears certain resemblances to, and at the same time, differs from, the European romantic hero. Chia Pao-yü is the traditional Chinese romantic hero par excellence. His basic nature is such that he has no respect for traditions or moral conventions. But neither does he become an outright rebel against society. Let us look more closely at Pao-yü. Raised in a large, wealthy, aristocratic household, he is a gifted child, "born with a piece of jade in his mouth" (rather like being "born with a silver spoon in his mouth") and shows literary talent at an early age. He is undoubtedly a *ts'ai-tzu*, i.e., a handsome, sensitive young man of literary talent. His constant companions are his numerous female cousins and their maidservants; he detests the company of men, particularly men of the official world. He considers them most vulgar. As he reaches manhood, Pao-yü shows little interest in Confucian learning or in an official career. His interests are in the otherworldly philosophies of Taoism and Buddhism. Moreover, he is inseparable from his equally temperamental, talented, and sensitive cousin Black Jade. However, the family decides that Black Jade, because of her poor health and erratic temperament, would not make a good wife for Pao-yü, and tricks him into marrying another cousin, Precious Virtue, who is even-tempered, pleasant, and sensible. Pao-yü literally loses his mind and his heart when he learns that his bride has been changed. And there are no alternatives in traditional Chinese society except to renounce this world, which Pao-yü eventually does. But before he does so, he must pass the state civil service examination, and have a son to continue the family name.[32]

In contrast to the European romantic hero, the Chinese romantic hero, owes a much greater debt to his family and society. While the former leaves his family early and lives by himself in isolation, the latter lives with his family and depends on his family even after marriage. Furthermore, the society provides the only legitimate means of achieving honor and recognition. Because of these close ties to his family and society, the Chinese hero's rebelliousness is less extreme, although his inner anguish may be just as great, if not greater, than that of his Western counterpart. The hero of *The Dream of the Red Chamber*, Chia Pao-yü, for example, certainly suffers greatly when he discovers that he has been deceived into marrying Precious Virtue, who is not his true love, but he must submit to the choice of the elders of the family, especially when it is the choice of his grandmother, the virtual head of the household. He despises the civil service examinations and official rank; nonetheless, he must sit for them in order to fulfill the expectations of the family. Finally, he must leave an offspring to continue the family line before he renounces the world of the Red Dust. He can rebel only after he has fulfilled his obligation to his family and society, not before. Therefore, his final revolt is tempered, but he has not suffered any less.

In his own words, Tseng P'u tells us that *Lu Nan-tzu* is "the grievous and painful cry of the whole of man's life. It is not merely the grief and pain of one man, but of all mankind. It is not the grief and pain of only a particular time, but of all time. . . . The whole of man's life is a vessel of pain. I have cast *Lu Nan-tzu* as a general model of such a vessel and let a few drops of blood seep out of it." [33] Tseng P'u's world view which underlines the pain and suffering of his hero Lu Nan-tzu consists of not only elements of Romanticism, but also the resignation of Buddhist philosophy—the acceptance of suffering as the basic element of human life, and a Zolaesque Naturalism of unceasing struggles against the environment.

Tseng P'u uses the Buddhist idea of *skandhas* to explain his theory of an outer-environment and an inner-environment. According to Buddhism, a person with all his "human baggage," his body, feelings, personality, etc., can be analyzed into five "heaps" or "constituents," technically known as the five *skandhas*. They are the *skandha* of Form (physical bodies), Feeling (pleasure, pain), Perceptions (sight, sound, . . .), Impulses (greed, hate, . . .), and Consciousness. [34] The "I" is a fictitious construct which has no real existence. Any event, such as a toothache, can be analyzed into these *skandhas*, and the statement "I have a toothache," then, becomes meaningless. Tseng P'u explains, "The outer-environment which I have mentioned corresponds to the *skandha* of physical forms. The inner-environment. . . corresponds to the *skandha* of perception and consciousness. Goodness and evil in conduct belong to the *skandha* of perception, and knowing belongs to the *skandha* of consciousness. In the same way that man cannot escape from the five *skandhas*, he cannot escape from his environment." [35]

The pain and suffering that man encounters in life are due to his futile struggles against these two kinds of environments: an outer-environment which consists of the family, society, politics, customs and habits, occupation, money, social class, etc.; and an inner-environment which consists of the seven emotions of joy, anger, sorrow, sensual pleasure, love, honor, and fear.

The struggle which takes place in man's life is based on the illusion that man can break away from his environment. But "the outer-enviroment is all around you, and continuously closing in on you. . . . Your soul, without your realizing it, subjects itself to the manipulations of the outer-environment and becomes its slave. . . ." [36] Struggle as hard as you may, you suffer only more pain in the end. Sometimes you cry out, "I have free will! I have power! I can overcome my environment!" But after breaking out of one environment, you merely find yourself in another. In fact, you cannot escape your environment; you are its prisoner.

Lu Nan-tzu is Tseng P'u's outcry at finding himself a prisoner of his environment. It is his expression of the weltschmerz. But by understanding it, perhaps he has transcended it.

CHAPTER 4

Nieh-hai hua, *A Political Novel*

I T is difficult to believe that *Lu Nan-tzu* and *A Flower in an Ocean of Sin* were written by the same author. Whereas *Lu Nan-tzu* (1929) is a westernized novel in the tradition of the French literary autobiographies, such as Stendhal's *Vie de Henry Brulard* or Chateaubriand's *Les Memoires d'outre-tombe*, *Flower* (1905) is an old-style prose narrative heavily burdened with traditional Chinese literary and cultural paraphernalia, such as the use of classical poetry in the text, couplet headings for the chapters, a scholar-beauty (*ts'ai-tzu chia-jen*) motif, and storyteller's remarks. In the intervening twenty years, from 1907 to 1927, Tseng P'u had changed from a traditional man of letters to a modern writer.

However, *Flower* is not by any means a solely traditional Chinese novel; it reflects the new trends and developments of late Ch'ing literature and society. The China that it depicts is not that of an unchanging China; rather, it is a China in great agitation, in a constant state of flux. Geographically, the scenes of the novel shift from Soochow, Shanghai, and Peking to Berlin and St. Petersburg; Bacon and Rousseau are juxtaposed with the famous Chinese poets Li Po (701–62) and Su Tung-p'o (1037–1101), Emperor Yang (reigned 604–618) of the Sui Dynasty with Louis XVI of France; the Chinese revolutionaries are juxtaposed with the Russian nihilists; the reformist philosophy of the Kung-yang school is contrasted to the revolutionary social philosophy of Saint-Simon; and the scholar-beauty romance is seen along with the passion of the nihilist lovers.

Although *Flower* is not a personal novel, it does reflect Tseng P'u's concern with the crisis in China and express his innermost feelings of doubt and ambivalence. If we believe with Leon Edel that the "subject selected by an artist more often than not reveals some emotion the writer had to express, some state of feeling, some view of life, some inner conflict or state of dis-equilibrium in his being, which sought resolution in the form of art,"[1] then *Flower* is the expression of Tseng P'u's feelings of pain and sympathy, anguish and impatience, marvel and astonishment which were transformed into the literary forms of tragedy, satire, and an odyssey.

I   *The Structure of* Flower

Flower is a panoramic novel about late Ch'ing society, which bears a certain resemblance to the Balzacian world of *La Comédie Humaine*. Although *Flower* can hardly equal the dimensions of *La Comédie Humaine*, its intention is certainly the same. Tseng P'u wrote in the preface to his revised edition of *Flower* that he wanted to record in cinematographic fashion the cultural and political changes that were taking place in China at a "flying pace" during the thirty years from 1870 to 1900. He mapped out for himself these thirty years of Chinese history in much the same way that Balzac staked out the Restoration period in French history. Because of Tseng P'u's panoramic design, Hu Shih and Ch'ien Hsüan-t'ung (1887–1939) in their famous debate on Chinese fiction criticized *Flower* and its author.[2]

In his criticism of *Flower*, Hu Shih made these charges against it: first, *Flower* reads more like a volume of casual notes than a novel; second, the author indulges in groundless superstition, thus revealing his "old fashioned muddle-headedness"; and third, the structure of *Flower* is loose, plotless, and episodic. In 1928, Tseng P'u wrote a preface for his revised edition of the novel in which he replied to Hu Shih's charges. As for the first point, Tseng P'u praised Hu Shih's perspicacity and admitted that he had tried to record as much as possible of the cultural and political changes that were taking place at the time, thus crowding the pages with people and events. As for the second point, Tseng P'u accused Hu Shih himself of old-fashioned muddle-headedness, and cited several examples of the use of fantasy and supernatural phenomena in Western literature. As for the last point on structure, which is of special interest to us here, Tseng P'u wrote:

As for Hu Shih's charge that the organization of *Flower* is like that of *The Scholars*[3] I dare not agree. Although a large number of brief accounts are used to make up the story (as is the case in *The Scholars*), the method of organization is drastically different. Let us take the analogy of stringing beads. The incidents in *The Scholars* are like beads strung straight through from beginning to end on one string. The end result is just one straight strand of beads. In my case, I coil and twist the string, this way and that; I tighten and loosen it, but never losing sight of the center. The end result is a string of beads in the shape of a flower. Or, let us take the analogy of flowers blossoming. The incidents in *The Scholars* are like flowers arranged in a single column, and they blossom sequentially from top to bottom. . . . In my case, I let the flowers blossom in the shape of an umbrella. Beginning in the center, they blossom in layers of different designs which bear a definite relationship to each other. The end product is a huge ball-shaped arrangement of flowers. . . . It cannot be said that my novel does not have a complex structure.[4]

Let us assume for the moment that there is a definite structure in *Flower*, but Tseng P'u's analogical characterization of it is not totally satisfactory. What does he mean specifically by "beads" and "flowers"? What "arrangement" is he talking about? The analogies do not give us these answers. But imprecise as these analogies may be, they do give us the clue to understanding the novel. The structure or organization of *Flower* is architectonically, or "spatially," laid out; i.e., the emphasis is on pattern and design, with a strong sense of proportion, symmetry, and balance rather than on unilinear plot development. This does not mean that there are no cause-and-effect relationships, character development, and so forth, but that these are subordinate to the principle of a "spatial" pattern or design. The narrative world depicted in this manner gives the author greater freedom to work with his materials and reduces the inexorableness of a unilinear plot. The technique of narration, or the "rhetoric" of the author, also comes into play here. What are the devices and techniques that the author uses to lay out the design, and how is it carried out? These questions we shall try to answer in this chapter.

It is very important to explain here that the edition of *Flower* used in this analysis is not the most commonly seen thirty-chapter revised and expanded edition. I have, instead, used the original twenty-four chapter unrevised version, twenty chapters of which were published in 1905, and five more, serially, in 1907 (but the last chapter was dropped from the twenty-four chapter edition). I have not used the revised thirty-chapter edition because Tseng P'u's later changes altered the tone and substance of the original, making it no longer a true late Ch'ing work and unsuited for our purposes. Also the death of Chin Wen-ch'ing in Chapter XXIV makes a natural break. I have dealt with the revised thirty chapter edition more extensively in the appendix.

The plot of the story tells of the rise and fall of the *chuang-yüan*, Chin Wen-ch'ing,[5] whose career can be divided into three stages. The first stage bridges about twenty years from his success in the Palace Examination in 1868 to his appointment as special minister to

Russia, Germany, Holland, and Austria in 1887. The second stage spans three years from 1887, when the protagonist boards the German ship S.S. *Saxon* for his mission abroad, to his appointment to the Tsungli Yamen in 1890 after his return to China. And the last stage is from 1890 after his return to Peking to his agonizing death in 1893. These three stages in the course of the *chuang-yüan's* development have three geographical centers of interest. The first is in Soochow, the second in Shanghai, and the third in Peking. Each of these cities has a special significance in the novel. They provide the background for the hero's climb to success. Soochow, for the Chinese, is synonymous with paradise on earth; its mild climate, beautiful women, elegant gardens, and natural landscape make it a scholar's dreamworld. The favorite pastime is to spend an evening on a boat on one of the many rivers and canals which crisscross the city. On the famous Seven-mile Canal, one can dine and watch the sunset, accompanied by charming, gifted courtesans who sing and chant poetry. In the novel it becomes the playground of the scholar-poet when he is in retirement.

In Shanghai the old meets the new, and the East meets the West. There is a constant bustle of activity; if it is not a flower exhibition in a public park, then it is a secret revolutionary meeting somewhere else. In the streets and public places, young men and women dressed in Western clothing are talking to foreigners in an alien tongue. Even dignified officials, wearing their long gowns and official caps, can be found dining in Western-style restaurants, eating with knives and forks, and drinking champagne and coffee. In their conversations, they talk about the government, politics, literature, and the arts of foreign countries. In the last decades of the Ch'ing dynasty, Shanghai was transformed from a busy trading port into the cosmopolitan, commercial center of China.

Peking is the stronghold of stubborn, reactionary forces. Tradition has a firm hold on its people, who are preoccupied with the glories of the past. Their ideal is the gentleman of leisure; erudition and expertise are prized for their own sake; courtesy, polite conversation, and refined manners are the sine qua non of social success. Holders of the three highest ranking honors in the Palace Examination (*chuang-yüan, pang-yen,* and *t'an-hua*), inhabit the world of Peking high society, and they make up the literati-aristocracy of Peking. They are obsessed by rare editions of ancient works, stone rubbings, paintings, and other treasures. Feasting and wine-drinking in the company of singing girls and boy-actors are common practices of the day. Their

love of wine, song, and poetry is only exceeded by their fondness for
objects of antiquity; and their fondness for objects of antiquity is only
exceeded by their love of gifted courtesans and boy-actors. Peking,
the capital of imperial China and the home of the literati-aristocracy,
is the principal setting of *Flower*.

Since we already have a general setting for the story, let us turn to
the hero and see how he is woven into the pattern, as it were. There
are two phases in the first stage of the action. In phase one, Chin, the
number one scholar in the empire, is faced with a dilemma: he is
uncertain of the value of the *chuang-yüan* in the unpredictable last
years of the Ch'ing dynasty. Although he is hailed as the *chuang-
yüan*, the title and honor which have been most coveted in Chinese
society for the past five hundred years, he is troubled by the changes
going on in the world around him. He feels inadequate. But first we
are given this tongue-in-cheek description of the *chuang-yüan*:

> . . . I think those of you who have not seen an explanation of the *chuang-yüan*
> do not know its true worth. China is the one and only nation in the world that
> has this institution, and there is only one *chuang-yüan* selected every three
> years. Only a person who has accumulated generations of merit, who is
> unmoved in the presence of beautiful women, who has close friendships in
> the capital, whose essays are·dazzling with elegance is qualified. He is the
> most outstanding among the immortals and a disciple of the Son of Heaven
> himself. He has such an air of nobility and wisdom about him that even Su
> Tung-p'o and Li T'ai-po must step back ninety *li* in deference. How much
> more so must Bacon and Rousseau! [6]

Following his success in Peking, Chin Wen-ch'ing asks for temporary leave to return to his home in Soochow. On the way he stops in
Shanghai where he greets many well-wishers and is entertained by
his friends. One of his well-wishers is Feng Kuei-fen (1809-1874), a
forceful, clear-headed modernizer who advises him to study "foreign
affairs," and exhorts him with the old adage "a scholar should feel
ashamed as long as there is one thing in the world of which he is
ignorant." That same evening his friend Hsüeh Shu-yün and five of
his colleagues in foreign affairs invite Chin for a Western-style dinner
at the restaurant I-p'in-hsiang. As he listens to his friends discourse
on the politics and learning of Western countries, he is brought to the
shameful realization that "Although I am a *chuang-yüan* and my
name is known throughout the empire, how can it be that I am
completely ignorant of these things. It is undreamt of! From now on,
it seems that high honors at the examinations do not amount to
anything. What is important is to learn about Western countries and

become an expert in foreign affairs, enter the Tsungli Yamen, and then obtain an appointment to go abroad. This is the only way to become famous." [7] While still in Shanghai, Chin has a brief encounter with the revolutionary Ch'en Ch'ien-ch'iu, who remarks, "I don't know how many promising young men have been ruined by these two words '*chuang-yüan*'."

After a brief stay in Soochow, Chin returns to Peking with his family. From this point on time passes quickly. Chin becomes an expert on foreign affairs by his own diligence on the one hand, and by recommendations of high officials in Peking on the other. In the process we are introduced to a gallery of characters in Peking, Kung Ho-fu, P'an Pa-ying, Li Ch'un-k'o, and others; for we are told that Peking is like a sea where one can find outstanding scholars in any field.

In the second phase there are two climaxes, the first of which is Chin Wen-ch'ing's meeting with the charming singing-girl, Fu Ts'ai-yün, who later becomes his concubine. This meeting between them is the first high point in the novel. It is the occasion for celebration, and in the course of it the pattern or design of the novel is laid out. Chin is persuaded by a number of his old friends to join them in celebrating the Ch'ing-ming Festival. Chin Wen-ch'ing joins them reluctantly as he is supposed to be in mourning for his mother who passed away nearly a year earlier. However, he becomes infatuated with the most beautiful of the singing-girls, Fu Ts'ai-yün, as soon as he sets eyes on her. The five friends, each accompanied by a singing-girl, board one of the renowned "flower boats" on the famous Ten-mile Canal in Soochow to view the sights and drink wine. It is truly one of those gatherings that is a happy blend of an appropriate setting, proper occasion, congenial company, and pleasant conversation, when:

> Bracelets move and hair-clasps fly,
> Flowers are fragrant and birds are singing.
> Music stirs the white silken handkerchiefs,
> And the wine is never enough.

The plot or design of the story is revealed in the following seven verses composed by the guests in a wine drinking game inspired by the prettiest singing-girl, Fu Ts'ai-yün. The first line of each verse must be from the text of the famous Ming dynasty drama *Mu-tan t'ing* (Return of the Soul or Peony Pavilion). The second line must be the name of an aria from the same drama, and the last line from the *Book of Poetry*. Then there is the special line which must be a verse from T'ang poetry which contains the two characters "*ts'ai*" and "*yün*," the characters of Fu Ts'ai-yün's name. The choice of the drama *Return of the Soul* is not accidental, since both *Flower* and the drama involve the return to life of heroines who had died. *Return of the Soul*, a long drama in fifty-five scenes by the sixteenth-century scholar-playwright, T'ang Hsien-tsu (1550–1616), tells of the love between Tu Li-niang, the daughter of a high official, and a young scholar, Liu Meng-mei, whom she meets and with whom she has an affair in a dream. Unable to have her dream fulfilled in real life, she pines away in lovesickness and is buried in the peony garden. Subsequently, the young scholar Liu comes upon her tomb; her spirit appears to him and urges him to open her coffin where he finds her alive and well. They marry, and after further obstacles the story ends with official promotion and a grand family reunion.

In the original, unrevised version of *Flower*, Chin Wen-ch'ing abandons a singing-girl whom he had befriended during his student days. Chin promises that he will return to marry her after he succeeds in the examinations. But when he fails to return, she commits suicide by hanging. Fifteen years later when he meets Fu Ts'ai-yün, there is at once a mutual fascination. Then he notices a red mark around her neck which she tells him she had at birth. When Chin next learns that she is aged fifteen, he realizes that she is the reincarnation of his former singing-girl; the red mark about her neck is the telltale sign of suicide by hanging in her previous existence. The parallelism between the two stories is meant to be more suggestive and symbolic than exact. Both heroines are charming and beautiful, and they both return to life. Here the similarity ends; the hero and heroine of the drama live happily ever after, whereas the lovers in *Flower* meet with tragedy.

Let us turn now to the seven poems.[8] The first verse reads:

> She stands like a cloud beside the moon;
> A gathering of worthy guests;
> They saunter about by the river.

And the crucial *fei-shang* or the "flying goblet" line, which must use the words *ts'ai* and *yün*, is:

> Ts'ai-yün and Hsiao-shih halt momentarily.

The first three lines describe the setting on the river, the gathering of guests, and Ts'ai-yün and Wen-ch'ing's being together for the first time at the banquet table. The last line tells of the sudden and immediate fascination with each other. Hsiao-shih, the legendary flute player who has magical powers to call forth dragons and phoenixes, of course, refers to the *chuang-yüan*, Wen-ch'ing. Throughout the verses, Ts'ai-yün has the double sense of literally meaning "beauty" and concretely referring to the heroine Fu Ts'ai-yün. This verse, then, sets the scene.

The second verse reads:

> Embarrassed by her shyness, she
>   fashions her hair aslant;
> Happy upon meeting;
> May the gentleman live for ten thousand years.

The *fei-shang* is:

> He learns to play the phoenix flute to
>   catch Ts'ai-yün.

These lines foretell their courtship and Chin's intention to take Ts'ai-yün as his concubine:

The third verse reads:

> Last night beyond the fragrant clouds;
> An audience at the Golden Gate;
> There is the sound of bells, regular and clear.

The *fei-shang* is:

> Stopping and starting, Ts'ai-yün continues to rise.

These lines foresee Wen-ch'ing's promotion to special minister to Russia, Germany, Holland, and Austria; and Fu Ts'ai-yün's elevation to first wife while she is abroad. The word "continues" refers to Fu Ts'ai-yün's rise from the position of a singing-girl to that of a *chuang-yüan*'s concubine, and finally to his wife.

The fourth verse reads:

> Afraid that she would be blown away by
>   "mist and rain";
> Remember me for my tenderness;
> We were to grow old together.

And the *fei-shang* is:

> Changes into Ts'ai-yün and flies away.

These lines forebode Fu Ts'ai-yün's amours in Europe, and her affair with the young German army officer, Count von Waldersee.

The fifth verse reads:

> In the vastness, hanging by clouds under
>   an autumn moon;
> A long way from home;
> The days and months will have gone.

The *fei-shang* reads:

> The song of the jade flute ends and
>   Ts'ai-yün is restless.

These lines forebode the end of Chin Wen-ch'ing's days; he dies soon after he returns from Europe. Fu Ts'ai-yün is impatient to move on to other amours.

The sixth verse reads:

> A picture of the conjugal pair in the azure sky;
> The highest tower;
> The wind whistles and the rain spatters.

The *fei-shang* reads:

> Ts'ai-yün dissolves easily and the colored
>   glass is thin.

Ironically, these lines composed by Chin Wen-ch'ing himself foretell the tragic end: Chin Wen-ch'ing's death and Fu Ts'ai-yün's departure from the Chin household.

The final verse reads:

> As soon as the traces of the "rain and mist"
>   have disappeared,
> Spring in the Jade Palace;
> Harmoniously we talked and laughed;

And the *fei-shang* is:

> Bundles up on the bridge, he grasps for Ts'ai-yün.

These last lines tell of the aftermath of the whole affair. After Chin Wen-ch'ing dies and Fu Ts'ai-yün leaves, only memories are left.

Now that we have the outline of the plot, let us see how the plot itself is carried out. In accordance with Verse III—"An audience at the Golden Gate;/There is the sound of bells, regular and clear";— Chin is appointed as ambassador to Europe shortly after he returns to Peking from Soochow. This is the ambition that he has cherished in his heart for more than ten years ever since he became a *chuang-yüan*. On the eve of his departure for Europe, he makes this pledge at a farewell banquet given by his friends: "I am not worthy of this appointment, and I need your advice. . . . The *Kuo-yü* (Conversation of the States) says, 'Know your opponent like yourself, and then you will have a hundred victories in a hundred battles.' Now we are at a disadvantage in our negotiations precisely because we do not know our opponent. If we do not know the condition of his country, it is harmful; but if we do not know his geography, it is disastrous! . . . I have for a long time devoted myself to a study of the geography of the northwest region, and perused all our records—they are all vague and confused. The Russians have always had designs on that region. . . . On my trip I dare not boast of any great accomplishments, but as for the geography of the northwest region, I shall not let my labors of the past twenty years go to waste. I am going to do an exhaustive study of that region and not let the Russians play any more tricks." [9] The first stage of the action ends with Chin's departure for Europe; furthermore, he has set his mind on making a name for himself in foreign affairs.

In the second stage of the action, there is a marked difference in the hero's ability to cope with his new environment. As soon as he is aboard the S.S. *Saxon*, his concubine Fu Ts'ai-yün becomes the center of attention, and Chin assumes a secondary role. In the first stage, Chin was on the upswing of the wheel of fortune. He has achieved the *chuang-yüan* title; he is respected and admired by his colleagues and fellow scholars; he has the support and backing of high officials in Peking. In his private life, he is as accomplished in wine-drinking, verse-making, and merry-making as he is in wielding a writing-brush in his official life. Under the old system, Chin was at ease and confident, and he had control over his actions. However, as soon as he leaves China, he is bewildered by a flood of new experiences and finds himself at a loss. While he is still on board the S.S. *Saxon*, he is swindled out of fifteen thousand marks for a blunder he has committed. Later in Germany, at an exorbitant price, he purchases twelve Sino-Russian border maps which are to help him settle boundary disputes, but these turn out to be faulty. In St. Petersburg while Chin is downstairs poring over his maps with great dedication, his concubine is having affairs upstairs.

The literati in general, and the *chuang-yüan* in particular, seem to take on comic roles. Lu Feng-ju, Chin's closest friend and a *chuang-yüan*, who is like the good-hearted Mr. Ma Erh of *The Scholars*, commits a faux pas in the home of the famous scholar-eccentric P'an Pa-ying. And even P'an himself is caught kowtowing to a pile of examination booklets of candidates whom he has failed. This is his way of easing his conscience for not passing all the deserving candidates. Even the *chuang-yüan* himself becomes the butt of comic farce. It is customary for a new *chuang-yüan* after his success to pay respects to all his examiners. But P'an, who is one of the examiners on this occasion, refuses to receive the new scholar because P'an had hoped the honor would go to someone else. Finally, after many attempts, the examiner favors his student with an appearance:

. . . When P'an suddenly appeared, looking very stern, the new candidate trembled and humbly knocked his head three times on the red carpet. The distinguished examiner acknowledged it with a slight wave of the hand. The candidate then nervously got up and backed unsurely on to a dais. The venerable one said, "Your essays are very good. Did you write them yourself?"

The candidate blushed crimson and answered, "Yes." The examiner then said, "You're very clever. I admire your skill." After which he had his servant bring tea for the candidate [a signal for the candidate to leave].

The candidate got up and backed off to go. But he did not notice that there were some steps in back of him. . . he slipped and fell over backwards with his four limbs thrashing in the air, . . . The venerable one guffawed and walked away. Needless to say, the candidate scrambled up and rushed for his carriage as quickly as possible.[10]

Interspersed with these comic episodes are several incidents of topical interest, such as Fu Ts'ai-yün's secret meeting with Queen Victoria II in Germany, and the episode about the Russian nihilists and their attempted assassination of Czar Alexander III. But the incidents in Peking make up the main sequence of events. The social gatherings in particular characterize Tseng P'u's technique. There is a small circle of Chin's friends, Lu Feng-ju, Ch'ien T'ang-ch'ing, and Chuang Hsiao-yen, who appear again and again on different occasions in the company of various people. Chin, of course, is the thread that links them together. However, when Chin is on his mission in Europe, it is his best friend Lu Feng-ju who becomes the connecting link; and Chin maintains contact with him by mail, telegram, and personal messenger.

In Chapter XI, Lu Feng-ju attends a celebration in honor of a famous Kung-yang commentator of the Han dynasty, Ho Shao (129–182), in the home of P'an Pa-ying. This celebration is, at the same time, a preparation for the grand birthday celebration for Li Ch'un-k'o in Chapter XX, the high point of the entire novel. There are nine guests besides the host himself, and they all appear again at the later gathering. Also, in Chapter XIII, after Lu Feng-ju has received the maps from Chin, he is invited by Ch'ien T'ang-ch'ing, another close friend of Chin, to a small party where Lu meets Tuan Hu-ch'iao, Chuang Hsiao-yen, and Wen Yün-kao, who also appear at the birthday celebration later. Lu gives the maps to Chuang Hsiao-yen, who is an official in the Tsungli Yamen, for safekeeping.

The climax of this section is the banquet at Wei-ch'un Garden in Shanghai shortly after Chin Wen-ch'ing returns to China. In spite of everything that has happened in the course of his mission, the honorable Chin Wen-ch'ing is hailed as a member of the new elite of foreign affairs experts. Recall the banquet given at the I-p'in-hsiang restaurant in Shanghai hosted by Hsüeh Shu-yün which took place some twenty years earlier; now he is the host again, and the six guests who were at that first meeting are all present again, including a few new ones. The size of the banquet has also increased from seven to eleven guests. This illustrates most clearly Tseng P'u's technique of "coiling and twisting the string but never losing sight of the center." Here we find the string crossing over itself after making a large loop. The guests talk nostagically about old times, and they discourse on the affairs of the world with their newly gained knowledge. Chin Wen-ch'ing, who felt such shame at their first meeting, now boasts of a personal message which he is bearing to the emperor from the Russian czar himself. This is the second high point in the novel.

Chin Wen-ch'ing has risen a step higher in the eyes of his colleagues, and soon he is to learn that he has been appointed to the Tsungli Yamen. This section ends when Chin is called away by a messenger from home.

The third part begins with Chin Wen-ch'ing's departure for Peking, after he learns that he has been appointed to the Tsungli Yamen. He arrives just in time for an elaborate birthday celebration for the famous, temperamental scholar-eccentric Li Ch'un-k'o, who is a veritable landmark on the Peking cultural scene. With eighteen guests, including high government officials, promising young scholars, provincial officials, and three favorite boy-actors of the guest of honor, plus poetry and song, this episode marks the climax of the novel and of Chin Wen-ch'ing's career. The host is Ch'eng Po-yi, an imperial clansman, who has a grand, luxurious private garden called Yün-wo Garden (Cloud Garden). The setting for this celebration is the most lavish of all those we have seen so far. The garden has a pond, pavilions, memorial arches, and lush natural vegetation. The magnificence of the occasion is also marked by the sheer number of guests; in addition, they are all men of talent and accomplishment. We have already met twelve of the eighteen guests on previous occasions.

After Li Ch'un-k'o has made a slow tour of the garden and has met all the guests, he and the host invite them all to sit down at the tables. The three boy-actors Ai-yün, Yi-yün, and Su-yün play their flutes and each sings an aria appropriate to the feast. Then the host suggests a drinking-game which requires verse-making in the Po-liang manner, that is, a poem in seven-syllable lines composed in succession by guests around the table. This Po-liang style, appropriately enough, was originated by the Emperor Wu (reigned 140–87 B.C.) of the Han dynasty to celebrate the completion of his magnificent Po-liang Tower in 108 B.C. Ch'eng further suggests that the verses be about each guest's most treasured object, such as rare books, stone rubbings, antiques, diaries, and paintings. The guest of honor, Li Ch'un-k'o, names his diary, which he has kept continuously for forty years. For

Chin Wen-ch'ing, it is his set of border maps, which he has purchased in Europe. For Chuang Hsiao-yen, it is his collection of paintings by Wang Shih-ku. Li Shih-nung names his collection of Hua-shan rubbings of the classics, and so on. After all eighteen guests have composed their verses, much wine has been consumed. Everyone is rosy-cheeked and merry, especially the guest of honor, Li Ch'un-k'o, who leaves the table with a boy-actor by his side to enjoy a tête-á-tête.

After this high point, the denouement begins. Chin Wen-ch'ing falls ill for a month; then his good friend Ch'ien T'ang-ch'ing brings the bad news that his maps have been used by the Russians to gain territory for themselves, and charges have been made against him. Also his concubine, Fu Ts'ai-yün, becomes restless in Peking and begins to take lovers. Then news arrives that P'an Pa-ying is seriously ill, and he dies soon afterwards. By Chapter XXIV, the border question involving the maps is settled and Chin Wen-ch'ing is absolved from blame. But his colleague Chuang Hsiao-yen insults him, and Fu Ts'ai-yün makes a cuckold of him by further indiscretions, so that he finally breaks down. Just before his death all his fears and wrongdoings come to haunt him in his hallucinations: Fu Ts'ai-yün's lover, the German officer Count von Waldersee; the ship's captain; his personal servant, A Fu; and finally, as he looks into Fu Ts'ai-yün's face, he sees the face of the singing-girl whom he had betrayed twenty years earlier. Chin cries out for help and loses consciousness. The workings of retribution or *karma* have come full circle and Chin dies.

The features of *Flower* which we have analyzed, the architectonic structure and the incremental dramatic development with banquets and celebrations, are not entirely new with Tseng P'u. The use of cryptic poems to lay out the design of the story occurs in Chapter V of *The Dream of the Red Chamber*,[11] where Chia Pao-yü, the hero of the novel, in his dream wanders into the Realm of the Great Void and discovers the registers of the Twelve Maidens of Chin-ling. These registers record the fate of Pao-yü's female cousins and maidservants, but he reads them without understanding. Then the Twelve Songs of the Red Chamber Dream are sung to Pao-yü, who listens without comprehension. These twelve songs, again in veiled language, relate the story of the novel. But they all fall on deaf ears. The careful reader of the novel, however, can catch the clues. As is the case in *Flower*, the protagonist remains ignorant of future events, while the reader is permitted a glimpse of what is to come.

We find the use of incremental dramatic development in the great

satirical novel *The Scholars (Ju-lin wai-shih).*[12] Banquets, poetry
parties, weddings, and operatic performances are placed at strategic
points in the novel which lead to the grand sacrificial ceremony at the
T'ai-po Temple in Chapter XXXVIII. Seventy-two distinguished
Confucian scholars, musicians, and worthy bohemian men of letters
are the principals at the grand ceremony. Spectators from miles
around, young and old, line the streets cheering and waving. The
climax at T'ai-po Temple is like the birthday party for Li Ch'un-k'o at
Cloud Garden in *Flower*.

Tseng P'u certainly utilized these two devices to full advantage in
his novel, thus lending it a unique structure that Hu Shih and Ch'ien
Hsüan-t'ung overlooked.

Flower clearly bears the marks of its time. Some sections are
mainly of topical interest, such as the fascination with the hypnotist
Pierre, Fu Ts'ai-yün's secret meeting with Queen Victoria II, and the
activities of the Russian anarchists, even though they do serve a
purpose, that is, in providing a new perspective of China in relation to
the rest of the world. But Tseng P'u's style is elegant and refined, and
he is at his best in the various banquet scenes. He slows and lingers in
places, and moves quickly in others. His style has a smooth-flowing
quality which shows his full mastery of the materials and reassures the
reader of the true nature and workings of the narrator's world. The
gentle wisdom of the narrator prepares the reader for the unexpected. An example of the narrator's helpfulness is when he tells us
before the fateful meeting between Chin Wen-ch'ing and Fu Ts'ai-
yün: "At this point quiescence has reached its limit and longs for
action; *yin* is exhausted and *yang* begins to rise. It is just this feeling of
restlessness that stirs up the accumulated merits and demerits of his
[Chin Wen-ch'ing's] past existences." It is the natural order of the
universe to swing from non-action to action, and from action back to
non-action. The internal logic of the narrator's world is a complex
network of relationships, such as interactions between characters,
some coincidental, others decreed by fate; lines of action which do
not cross, or non-interactions; and other pure non-incidents. This
network is like a complex passageway which invites the visitor to
explore in a leisurely way its hidden recesses. This mode of narration,
in conjunction with the architectonic structure and incremental development, permits the Chinese author, by order of *its* internal logic,
to embrace a much greater variety of subject matter harmoniously
than is the case with modern Western novels. Causal sequences and
cause-and-effect relationships in general are not the only kinds of
logic at the Chinese storyteller's disposal.

II   *The Tragedy of the Chuang-yüan*

Flower was written in 1904, seven years before the Chinese Rev-
lution of 1911, when signs of the decay and disintegration of Chinese
society had become all too evident. Three incidents in particular
during the last decade of the nineteenth century revealed China's
weakness. Her defeat in the Sino-Japanese War of 1894–95 showed
the bankruptcy of official policy and the Self-strengthening program.
The reform effort which culminated in the Hundred Day's Reform
Movement of 1898 showed the failure of China's traditional intellectuals to effect a change from within. And the Boxer Uprising of 1900
showed the helplessness of indigenous groups, such as the secret
societies and other reactionary elements, to counter the influence of
foreigners on Chinese soil by violence. The officials of the government bureaucracy and the military forces had long ago lost their
moral fiber; licentiousness, corruption, and inertia marked their
conduct. It became evident that aside from foreign encroachments
which threatened her territorial integrity, China was deteriorating
from within. The fate of China depended on a number of well-
intentioned but inept high-level officials in Peking.

In the novel, Chin Wen-ch'ing, the protagonist and *chuang-yüan*
of 1868, is one of these high-level officials. His rise and fall is a
miniature of China's rise and fall. Since China's weakness at the time
was seen as the cumulative result of centuries of oppression, exploita-
tion of the common people, and general neglect of their welfare by
the ruling elite, Tseng P'u appropriately chose the inexorable force of
retribution as the theme of his novel. He skillfully identified the fate
of "a scholar with the highest honors (*chin-pang chuang-yüan*)" with
the fate of China. In the title of the novel, *Nieh-hai hua*, the "hua" or
"flower" stands for China in her past splendor; it also stands for the
chuang-yüan, for the beautiful courtesan who becomes the *chuang-
yüan's* concubine, and for the literati-aristocracy in Peking. The
nieh-hai or "ocean of sin" stands for all the injustices, corruption, and
evils which have been perpetrated by the past officials and rulers of
China. The extravagance and gaiety described in *Flower* are like an
Indian summer signaling the inevitable coming of severe weather.

In following Chin Wen-ch'ing's twenty-five years of scholarly and
political endeavors, from his rise to a *chuang-yüan* in 1868 to his
death in 1893, we come to understand him not merely as a symbol but
also as a man, a human being, living in unpropitious times. His
industry and learning in classical scholarship do not benefit him when
he is overseas. Once out of China, his concubine and personal ser-

vant, not to speak of others, deceive him and lord it over him. The death of Chin Wen-ch'ing is a personal tragedy as well as a social one. It is precisely his dual roles as a refined Chinese gentleman of learning and a complete misfit and bungling minister overseas that make him a tragic figure.

Chin Wen-ch'ing belongs to the social and political elite in the mainstream of traditional Chinese society, and he has had a distinguished public career. Moreover, he is not a bookish pedant. In his private life, he was once a winsome gentleman skilled in poetry and the wine-cup. As a promising young scholar, he frequented the courtesans' quarters; even in middle age he takes a fifteen-year-old courtesan as his concubine. If times had not changed, he would have ended his days in security and comfort. But in a rapidly changing world his position is jeopardized. When he is in Germany and Russia, his concubine dominates the spotlight while he cowers in his study with his books and lets his official duties go untended for days. Although he has ambitions of protecting China's national boundaries, his abilities are not commensurate with these aims. His crowning achievement in his own eyes, the purchase of a set of Sino-Russian border maps, turns out to be the cause of his downfall. The maps are inaccurate, and in negotiating with the Russians they are used to China's disadvantage. He is consequently disgraced.

Chin Wen-ch'ing's downfall and death symbolize the passing of the traditional Chinese literati-aristocracy. The whole class dies because of its bookish impracticality, its general misconception and miscalculation of the world, and its excessive pride in name and reputation. Its fall is, at the same time, the fall of traditional China.

The overall form of the novel is a tragic one. From the very beginning, we are not allowed any illusions about the state of affairs in China in the last years of the Manchu dynasty. The prologue to the novel describes an out-of-the-way island called the Island of Enslaved Happiness (Nu-lo tao) where the inhabitants live a carefree, ignorant, savage existence without ever taking one breath of the air of freedom. One day the island begins to sink into the sea. But, lo and behold, the Island of Enslaved Happiness is really connected to Shanghai! This out-of-the-way place is really China herself. On a more realistic level, an observer in the novel then takes note of Japanese encroachments in Manchuria, "Not only is Manchuria in danger, but the whole of China is about to be lost!" It is just this contrast of impending disaster with the gaiety and extravagance of the banquets and celebrations that creates the inexorable sense of doom in the novel. We have seen how the festivities become larger and larger, more and more lavish as the principals move from Soochow to Shanghai, and from Shanghai to Peking. Chin Wen-ch'ing's career also advances with the progression of the banquets, but in reality his competence and ability are not in step with his outward success. We are certain that he will fall also.

The tragedy of Chin Wen-ch'ing is not a heroic tragedy; it is rather an ironic or social tragedy in which the protagonist's power of action does not rise above the forces of his environment. Unable to overcome these forces, he becomes their prisoner and victim. Although the working of retribution is the motivating principle of this tragedy, the overall sweep of the action does not implicate clear-cut villains nor reward victims. *Flower* comes to an end without a sense of resolution. Chin has simply passed on with the movement of the *yin* and *yang*.

III   *The Satiric World of* Flower

Flower is written in the satiric mode. The target of Tseng P'u's satiric attack is not only Chin Wen-ch'ing, but the whole complex of the examination system which includes, in addition to the literati, the government bureaucracy and the various forms of corruption and immorality created by the examination ethos. Again, China's disordered internal conditions at the end of the nineteenth century and the theme of the novel itself suggest a preoccupation with the morbid, the grotesque, the seamy, and the ridiculous side of society. The polemical tools that Tseng P'u brings to bear range from subtle irony, on the one hand, to outright vituperation on the other, passing through the intermediate stages of satire and sarcasm.

The main narrative about Chin Wen-ch'ing and his concubine Fu Ts'ai-yün is interspersed with anecdotes about different aspects of society. For example, there are descriptions of desperate, trembling *Hanlin* scholars sitting for examinations at the imperial palace; the romance of a Manchu nobleman with a flowerboat girl in Soochow; the meteoric rise of an official from poverty to riches and power by his ruthless memorializing; the efforts of Ta-tao Wang Erh, a Robin Hood figure, to right singlehandedly overwhelming injustices, and a grotesque episode about a lowly treasury attendant who tries to secure high public office through bribery, but is totally illiterate. These anecdotes are selected commentaries on the times.

Tseng P'u harshly indicts the time-honored examination system in these words:

Can you guess what is this thing called the "examinations"? . . . Why must we have it? Alas! This is a most heartbreaking story. After having suffered from its evils for over a thousand years, we are still unwilling to wake up. We still refer to it as the "magnificent favor" or the "sacred rites."

Rubbish! What "magnificent favor!" What "sacred rites!" Autocratic rulers devised this most perverse method to bind a people. The examination halls are like dungeons. The eight-legged essays and tests are inhuman instruments of torture. The rankings for the students are forms of punishment.

After the examinations were introduced into our country, our people became soulless thinking machines and spiritless bodies. The great realm of the Middle Kingdom became the hereditary property of the rulers; and we, the people, descendants of the former sage-kings, became nothing but slaves of the rulers. The rulers do what they please without any regard for the people. Now that a barbarian people is ruling our country, and our strength is being sapped, we still keep on dreaming our sweet dreams! [13]

This passage has frequently been cited to show the revolutionary zeal of its author. It clearly expresses an anti-Manchu sentiment, but it is not characteristic of the novel as a whole. In fact, Tseng P'u's method is more often subtle, anecdotal, oblique, with a sense of amusement, rather than vituperative.

Take as an example Tseng P'u's comment on the importance of ink in the examinations. "Rank and honor completely depend on it. If the ink is ground to precisely the right consistency, then the characters written with it will be fat and sleek. When the examiner reads them he will be pleased. On the other hand, if the ink is not ground to the right consistency, then the characters written with it will look lean and faded. The examiner will not be pleased, and the scholar will remain a poor *Hanlin* all his life. Therefore, the *Hanlin*'s ink is as important as the prime minister's ability to cook soup." [14] In the last years of the dynasty, when appearances counted so much more than substance, a scholar's writing could be judged on the basis of his calligraphy rather than the content.

In another anecdote about a *Hanlin* scholar, Chuang Shou-hsiang (modelled on Chang Chih-tung), Tseng P'u tells how he almost fails to produce an essay at a general examination. He is described as short, ape-like in appearance, with an oily, stubble beard, but he is a man of broad learning and great literary skill. During the examinations, others ask him questions and he answers energetically, gesticulating vigorously all the time. But when the examination is about to end, he still has not written a line. He calls to his friends in desperation, "Please help me put something together and get it over with!" His friends gather around him; someone rules his paper; another grinds his ink; a third holds the candle; and a fourth chooses the appropriate words for him. After a while, he manages to scrape an essay together, and leaves with a sigh of relief. Obviously the examinations have lost all significance to Chuang and all scholars like him.

Another anecdote is about corruption on the level of the lowly and ignorant. Even a completely illiterate treasury attendant who has been trained to smuggle gold and silver from the treasury by stuffing gold coins up his intestinal tract hopes to secure office through special favor. At an audience before the Empress Dowager, when the treasury attendant is asked to write down an account of himself, he turns white and glassy-eyed as if he had been sentenced to death. He picks up the writing brush, holds it over the paper, and hesitates for a long time. Beads of sweat roll down his nose, but no characters appear on the paper. After several minutes, the Empress Dowager says, "Since you can't write in Chinese, then write in your own Manchu language. You certainly have not forgotten it!"

The unfortunate Mr. Yü had never read a book nor seen a character since the day he was born. He held the writing-brush like a foreigner holding chopsticks for the first time. How could he write! The Empress Dowager laughed sarcastically and said, "Dismissed! You'd better return to your post as treasury attendant."

As soon as he heard this, the honorable Mr. Yü, who was just then wishing for a hole to crawl into, thanked Her Majesty profusely, and scurried away like an oversized rat.[15]

The satiric world of *Flower* contains many other episodes which need not be mentioned here. They illustrate the chicanery, corruption, and shamelessness of officials from senior ministers to illiterate clerks. They drive home the truth of the Chinese adage, "If the main beam is not straight, then the whole house will be crooked," and testify to the true satiric spirit. In Alvin Kernan's theory of the satiric scene, he says, "The scene of satire is always disorderly and crowded, packed to the very point of bursting. The deformed faces of depravity, stupidity, greed, venality, ignorance, and maliciousness group closely together for a moment, stare boldly out at us, break up, and another tight knot of figures collects. . . . Everywhere the satirist turns he finds idiocy, foolishness, depravity, and dirt."[16] We find that the Chinese satirist is in full agreement with his counterpart in the West.

IV A New Perspective on China

In times of disorder, men have embraced an alien religion, a foreign philosophy, or a new world vision to give unity and coherence to their otherwise chaotic experience. In the last half of the nineteenth century the traditional Chinese world order was breaking down. The intrusion of Western "barbarians" brought chaos and disorder into the lives of the people. China could no longer be defined in the ethnocentric terms of a culturally superior center surrounded by concentric spheres of peoples of lower cultural levels fanning out to the peripheral regions of utter barbarism. The central position occupied by the Chinese state and the Chinese people had to give way to a more pluralistic world in which China occupied only a small part. How does this altered view of the world affect Tseng P'u's narrative world? How does he deal with the traditional Chinese world order? How does he play off native Chinese values and concepts against foreign ones?

Tseng P'u's *Flower* is one of the few late Ch'ing works that deals substantively with the outside world, foreign lands, ideas, and peoples. There are a few works, such as Li Po-yüan's *Wen-ming hsiao-shih* (A Brief History of Civilization, or Modern Times) which deals tangentially with a foreign missionary in one of its episodes, and *K'u she-hui* (Bitter World) which is about the suffering of Chinese overseas set in the background of the United States. But these descriptions of character and place are very sketchy. Only Tseng P'u's *Flower* makes the people and places in foreign lands come alive. How successful his venture is still is under debate, but Tseng P'u did make an earnest attempt to integrate China into the global scene, or to fit the Western world into the Chinese world order.

In the novel, Western ideas and experiences are transformed into an odyssey as Chin Wen-ch'ing and his concubine, Ts'ai-yün, make their tour of European countries. The travelers are alternately astonished and fascinated by magicians, hypnotists, Western beauties, revolutionary ideas, and especially, the Russian nihilists. The revolutionary activities of the nihilists struck a sympathetic chord in the hearts of progressive Chinese intellectuals because the Chinese were just beginning their own revolution. The odyssey is at the same time an educational tour on which the Chinese not only learn about Western countries, but also learn about themselves, and assimilate their own historical development into a world pattern.

Tseng P'u's treatment of the Russian anarchists occupies two chapters in which he takes the incidents about the nihilist heroine, Hsia-ya-li (Sarah Aizenson ?), [17] and weaves them into an exotic tale of love and romance, intrigue and mystery, and selfless heroism. Sarah is a girl of striking beauty and intelligence. She knows more than ten languages, including Chinese. She lived in China for three years. As a young woman, she decides to dedicate herself to driving out the czar and overthrowing his government. She secretly joins an underground nihilist group, then sacrifices her personal happiness and her own lover to marry a wealthy man whom she despises in order to secure funds for her party. Finally, she gives up her life in an attempt to assassinate the czar.

Chin Wen-ch'ing meets her for the first time on the S.S. *Saxon* and is at once struck by her beauty:

She was about twenty, the very epitome of a Western beauty. She wore a black dress, a matted straw hat, and dark glasses. Although she was dressed very plainly, her fair skin, golden hair, long eyebrows, slender waist, blue eyes, and red lips conveyed a picture of indescribable beauty. As she looked on, leaning lazily against the door, she stole the heart of our ambassador Chin. [18]

She has been in China for three years and is just returning to her own country. Tseng P'u describes the Russian nihilists in purely idealistic and romantic terms. The young men and women are all beautiful and talented. In their eyes, duty and honor to country come above all else.

Compare the nihilist heroine with the Chinese concubine and we have a dramatic contrast between the ultimate in the modern liberated woman of the West and the most tradition-bound woman of the East. As she pulls out her shining pistol about to shoot Ambassador Chin for having had her hypnotized, Sarah says, "I want to ask you: since we have no grudges against each other, why have you played this trick on me? Don't you realize that I am a well-known figure in Russia, and totally unlike your submissive Chinese woman who feels no shame on being treated as a toy . . ."

As we know, Fu Ts'ai-yün is a far cry from the stereotyped, submissive, Chinese woman; she is shrewd and capable, ever watchful for an opportunity to enhance herself. She would later become the famous courtesan Sai-chin-hua. Ts'ai-yün knows her social status and plays her role accordingly when the circumstances dictate it. But she essentially declares her independence in Chapter XXI in an argument with Chin Wen-ch'ing. Sarah and Ts'ai-yün are both beautiful and talented women, each in her own way, but their backgrounds and environments cause them to be worlds apart.

The ideology of the Russian nihilists is revealed to Ambassador Chin by a friend of Sarah's, Pierre, who is also on the S.S. *Saxon*. Chin shudders as he listens to Pierre say,

". . . The organization to which Sarah belongs was founded by the Frenchman Saint-Simon, a believer in true equality. He believes that all talk about equality is superficial. . . . The aim of his organization is to turn this false equality into genuine equality, to break down all national, social, racial, family, and religious barriers. Rulers are enemies of the people; governments are bandits and robbers. National affairs should be decided upon and managed by all the people. And the land of the country should be like a public park; the financial resources of the country should be enjoyed by all. Ten thousand people should act as if they have only one soul, and ten thousand souls should act as if they have only one goal. This is the way to seek the new world of complete equality. . . ."

Wen-ch'ing uttered in alarm, "But this is going against the Way of Heaven, and seditious . . ."

Pierre countered, " . . . It is the emperor who is guilty of 'Going against the Way of Heaven,' and not the people. And if the emperor can be seditious, why can't the people? The land belongs to the people; the government belongs to the people; the people are the ones in charge. The emperor and the government are public servants, that is all. . . ." [19]

Ambassador Chin wants to object but thinks it best to remain silent and not make any more trouble.

Not quite as outspoken as the Saint-Simonians, but just as revolutionary in the Chinese context, were the ideas of the Kung-yang school of reform. This school was based on a reexamination of the ideas of Confucius and reinterpretation of the Confucian classics which permitted and sanctioned reform and the ideas of evolutionary change and progress in Chinese society. This was an important ideological breakthrough, even if it only mustered limited support. Under its chief spokesman, K'ang Yu-wei, the school first attacked the authenticity of the classics, then argued that Confucius really wanted to change the institutions of the Chou dynasty rather than follow them, and, finally, reinterpreted certain passages from the *Kung-yang Commentary* (hence the name Kung-yang school) and the *Record of Rites* (*Li chi*) and derived a three-stage evolutionary theory of social change. The first stage was the Age of Disorder, second, the

Age of Approaching Peace and Tranquility, and third, the Age of Great Peace and Unity. According to K'ang, China and the world were about to enter the Age of Approaching Peace and Tranquility if his reforms were instituted. And under the Age of Great Peace and Unity there would be one world united under one government where men and women would live in complete freedom and equality, and all the suffering created by national, racial, and class barriers would be removed. Although this school of thought did not take hold in China, it did disturb the complacency of the Confucian officials.

But soon these ideas were superseded by those of the revolutionaries who advocated assassination and violent overthrow of the Manchu government. Reform was too slow for them. The close parallel between the Russian anarchists and the Chinese revolutionaries was part of the new consciousness of the Chinese. The anarchists and revolutionaries may differ in their ideologies, but their tactics of assassination, armed insurrection, and wholehearted dedication to social and political ideals, were identical. The new world view of *Flower* is a bizarre mixture of new ideas and values yet to be coherently integrated into the changing Chinese world view.

As we turn the pages of the novel, we notice many changes in mood and tone. The novel begins with condemnation, then moves to cynicism and satire. The panorama of life in China and Europe, described in Chapters VIII–XIX, must have been a source of fascination for the Chinese reading public at the time. And the fact that most of the characters are thinly disguised characterizations of well-known public figures in real life, must have added an extra dimension to the enjoyment of the novel. The theme of retribution forms the scaffolding or superstructure which gives *Flower* its forcefulness and unity. The fate of the *chuang-yüan* coincides with the imminent fate of imperial China. The frustration of the social tragedy finds temporary relief in satire and irony. The new world view of *Flower* puts China and her fate into a new perspective, thus giving her people a new perception and consciousness about themselves.

CHAPTER 5

Nieh-hai hua *and the Late Ch'ing World*

I N 1927 Tseng P'u wrote that *A Flower in an Ocean of Sin* was "a lucky child; as soon as it was published, contrary to expectations, it was warmly received by society. It was reprinted fifteen times, and no less than 50,000 copies were sold. There were praises, studies, imitations, and continuations. Who knows how much ink was spilt over it; how many printing blocks were ruined over it." [1] True, soon after its publication, *Flower* engendered a proliferation of studies, commentaries, criticisms, continuations, and adaptations. [2] Among the continuations were those by Lu Shih-e, Ch'ü Yüan, T'ien-hsiao-sheng, T'ien-pao-kung-jen, Chang Hung, and Hsia Yen. [3] Criticisms of *Flower* abounded. Among the notable early ones were those by Hu Shih and Lu Hsün. Hu Shih was unfavorable and Lu Hsün favorable. The disagreements over the novel were not only due to the nature of the novel itself, but also reflected cultural and ideological conflict.

In an exchange of letters between Hu Shih and Ch'ien Hsüan-t'ung in 1917, Hu Shih wrote, "*Flower* I regard as a second-rate novel, which should not be grouped together with *Water Margin, The Dream of the Red Chamber, The Scholars, The Bureaucracy Exposed*, and *Strange Events Witnessed in the Past Twenty Years*. As a record of events of the recent past, it is excellent. But, as a novel, its plot is loosely joined together; it tries to include too much, thus becoming more suitable as a volume of notes than a novel." [4] With regard to its contents, Hu Shih believed that *Flower* was written "without the realization that prostitution and concubinage were despicable matters . . . . A hundred years from now when our moral standards have been raised to a higher level, . . . and if American readers were to read these novels, they would be shocked." [5] Clearly, Hu Shih had taken nonliterary factors into consideration, and his literary frame of reference is that of the Western reader rather than the Chinese reader. His views on the plot of *Flower*, again, appear to be derived from modern Western concepts, those of Gustave Flaubert and Henry James. Hu Shih's views of the novel definitely reflected the influence of his Western educational background.

Lu Hsün, on the other hand, working from the point of view of a Chinese literary historian, succinctly observed that late Ch'ing fiction was the direct result of contemporary political and social conditions. He wrote in his *Brief History of Chinese Fiction*: "During the nineteenth century, though many internal uprisings were suppressed, including the White Lotus, T'ai-p'ing, Nien, and Hui, China suffered defeat at the hands of the foreign powers, such as Britain, France, and Japan. . . . Two years after the failure of the Hundred Days Reform of 1898 came the Boxer Uprising which was the result of the people's realization of the powerlessness of the government. Therefore, the trend in fiction was to expose the abuses, lash out at the government, and criticize social conventions. Similar to the earlier satirical works, these novels' intended purpose was to aid in setting the world aright. But in these works, the criticisms were made brazenly with no subtlety, and were exaggerated to suit the popular taste." [6] Lu Hsün categorized the works of this period as "castigatory fiction" (*ch'ien-tse hsiao-shuo*). Then he singled out four works which he considered most representative of this trend: Li Pao-chia's *The Bureaucracy Exposed*, Wu Wo-yao's *Strange Events*, Liu E's *The Travels of Lao Ts'an*, and Tseng P'u's *Flower*. While noting their common tendency to exaggerate, Lu Hsün characterized *Flower* as a novel with a "compact and well-conceived plot and an elegant style." It excelled in its "descriptions of high officials and men of letters of the time." Reflecting more traditional Chinese aesthetic values, Lu Hsün readily accepted the plot-structure of *Flower* which was generically different from the modern Western conception. This I have tried to show in the previous chapter. Unfortunately, Lu Hsün did not elaborate on his statement about the plot of *Flower*. It would have been most useful had he done so.

The cultural and ideological conflicts between Hu Shih and Lu Hsün, however, account only partially for their different points of view. Even within the same ideological camp there are differences of opinion. In 1956, Ch'en Tse-kuang of Sun Yat-sen University hailed *Flower*, in spite of its ambivalences and limitations, as the "best revolutionary novel of the late Ch'ing period" because it embodied the ideas of the bourgeois democratic revolution.[7] A Ying and Chang Pi-lai had earlier expressed a similar view.[8] Ch'en also noted that the novel was strongly anti-imperialist, anti-feudal, and patriotic. Eight years later, in 1964, Ko Chieh took issue with this view.[9] He claimed that *Flower* was not in favor of the bourgeois democratic revolution; it was only a bourgeois reformist novel. He pointed out that Tseng P'u's descriptions of revolutionaries, such as Ch'en Ch'ien-ch'iu, Shih Chien-ju, and Sun Yat-sen, were superficial, stereotyped, and lifeless. They lacked the depth of feeling found in his characterization of bureaucratic officials and traditional men of letters. Ko also noted that Tseng P'u's condemnation of feudal institutions was ambiguous because his criticisms were a mixture of love and hate which left the reader with mixed feelings. Tseng P'u's preoccupation with sexual innuendo and sensational gossip were also cited as serious flaws. At a time when the bourgeois democratic revolution was at its height, Tseng P'u supported only the reformist view, thus making the novel reactionary and backward, therefore not deserving praise.

Among other things these conflicting views of *Flower* indicate that the novel itself may be ambiguous. It may embody Tseng P'u's own love-hate relationship with the past. After all, he grew up in the old society and enjoyed its privileges before abandoning it. He associated with the crème de la crème of the old society. In the novel, a significant portion of the main characters were his personal acquaintances, some even members of his family. Ts'ao Kung-fang (Tseng Chih-chuan) was his father; Ch'ien T'ang-ch'ing (Wang Ming-luan) was his father-in-law; Kung Ho-fu (Weng T'ung-ho) was a close friend of the family; Chin Wen-ch'ing (Hung Chün) and Fu Ts'ai-yün (Sai-chin-hua) were also Tseng P'u's friends.

Tseng P'u tells us that in 1892 he frequently visited Hung Chün in his home and met his attractive concubine, Sai-chin-hua: "I met Sai-chin-hua for the first time in Peking. At the time I was holding the post of a secretary of the Grand Secretariat. I went to the Hungs' home often and met Sai-Chin-hua many times. She carried herself with poise; her eyes were very lively. She did not speak often, but communicated with her eyes and movements as if she spoke to you. For example, if there were ten people at the table eating, she would use her hands, eyes, and lips to make all the ten people feel happy and satisfied; no one felt left out. She was not a great beauty, but her features were pleasing. She was generous and informal in dealing with people and made friends easily."[10] Hung Chün died in October, 1893, and his family left Peking. But these two people were to leave a lasting impression on Tseng P'u and became immortalized in the pages of his novel. At this point, a brief look at late Ch'ing fiction as a whole and the circumstances surrounding the creation of *Flower* are in order.

I   *Late Ch'ing Fiction (1900–1911)*

Until fairly recently, late Ch'ing novels have generally been disparaged because of their supposedly intolerant, vituperative, exaggerated, and muckraking style. Lu Hsün characterized these novels as castigatory fiction in his *A Brief History of Chinese Fiction* in 1924. Although this term is now recognized to be a misnomer, its legacy has remained.

It cannot be denied, however, that there are some justifications for Lu Hsün's view. The political and social circumstances of the time called for a highly inflammatory literature. The many political and military setbacks that China had suffered in her confrontation with the West, and the social injustices and corruption of the officials internally, all added up, in the people's eyes, to a chaotic and powerless government. The disappointment, discontent, and pent-up emotions found expression in the literature of the time. Furthermore, this literature, especially the fiction, was often not written by the traditional gentlemen-scholars, like Ts'ao Hsüeh-ch'in (ca. 1716–1763), Wu Ching-tzu (1701–1754), or Li Ju-chen (1763–ca. 1830) who spent a lifetime perfecting one opus. The new writers of the late Ch'ing period often wrote for a living. They had the fundamentals of a classical education, but were disillusioned with the traditional institutions of social mobility and turned to other occupations. Li Pao-chia (1867–1906) and Wu Wo-yao (1867–1910) were typical examples of this new kind of journalist-littérateur. They were both prolific writers who wrote for and were editors of literary magazines. Most of their works were first serialized in magazines and newspapers before they were published in book form. These men, under the pressures of time, wrote hurriedly and produced works that had to meet the demands of their reading public. Therefore, these new works generally tended to lack the refinement and subtlety of the earlier novels, and hence deserved to some extent the term castigatory.

With the passage of time and changes in perspective, some present-day scholars are once more turning to this large body of late Ch'ing literature with renewed interest. Upon closer examination, these commonly labelled "castigatory" novels are not all found to derserve that particular label. There is surprising variety, vigor, and innovation in some of them. Spearheading a systematic reevaluation of late Ch'ing fiction is a small group of scholars under the guidance of Milena Dole elová-Velingerová at the University of Toronto.[11] Their studies clearly reveal that, both in terms of subject-matter and technique, these novels represent a transitional phase. In particular,

structural and narrative innovations presaged later literary developments of the May Fourth period.

To give some idea of the quantity and variety of works produced
during these last ten years of the late Ch'ing period, in fiction alone
four to five hundred novels were published.[12] (This figure does not
include Chinese translations of Western works, nor works in the
other genres of poetry and drama which also number in the hundreds.) They range from the more traditional historical romances and
scholar-beauty novels to Sherlock Holmes mysteries and the new
novels of love and sentiment, and even science-fiction-like utopian
works. But the most distinctive features of these works were their
sense of social involvement and ideological commitment. Social and
political themes on the exposure of the life of officials were most
popular. But works on the liberation of women, the issue of constitutional government, the anti-Manchu movement, competition in the
world of business and industry were also numerous. There were also
novels on life in America and novels attacking the anti-Chinese
immigration laws of 1905. Others were frequently directed against
superstition and popular customs and habits.[13] This literature thus
recorded the bankruptcy of the old order and the sense of crisis and
bewilderment of the younger generation.

The reasons for this phenomenal literary outburst were many;
modern methods of printing and publishing; a sizable middle-class
reading public which had developed in the large urban centers; the
existing political conditions which were intolerable; a new conception
of language and literature; the influence of Western literature; and a
phenomenal growth in the number of magazines and newspapers in
print. The situation is too complex to be fully explained here.[14]
Suffice it to say that these conditions, directly and indirectly, had
their influence on Tseng P'u and his writing of *Flower*.

II *The Writing of* Flower

When *Flower* was published in February, 1905, the title page read
"Originated by the Lover of Freedom" (Ai-tzu-yu che ch'i-fa) and
"Edited and told by the Sick Man of East Asia" (Tung-ya ping-fu
pien-shu). The Sick Man of East Asia, of course, was Tseng P'u, but
the identity of the Lover of Freedom was not publicly revealed until
1928 in Tseng P'u's preface to his revised edition of *Flower*.

The Lover of Freedom was the pen name of Chin Sung-ts'en

(1874–1947), or Chin I, also named T'ien-yü, a younger contemporary of Tseng P'u. During the late Ch'ing period, he was a political activist who had joined the Patriotic School (*Ai-kuo hsüeh-she*) with Tsou Jung (1885–1905), Chang Ping-lin (1868–1936), Ts'ai Yüan-p'ei (1867–1940), and others who advocated the overthrow of the Manchu government. During this period he wrote essays on the relationship between fiction and society, translated a work on the Russian nihilists called *Tzu-yu hsüeh* (The Blood of Freedom), and an autobiographical work by the Japanese adventurer Mayazaki Torazō called *San-shih-san nien lo-hua meng* (A Thirty-three Year Dream of Falling Flowers).[15] In 1903 in response to requests by Chinese students in Japan soliciting materials for their magazine *Kiangsu* (1903–1904), Chin Sung-ts'en wrote several chapters of a novel called *Nieh-hai hua*, two chapters of which were published in that magazine. As to how the subject-matter of his novel was chosen, Chin Sung-ts'en said in an interview in 1934: "Because China was just then interested in Russia and several anti-Russian societies were being organized, I chose to write about Hung Wen-ch'ing, who was the special minister to Russia, and his concubine Sai-chin-hua [who accompanied him]. They were chosen not at random, but because of their importance in Sino-Russian relations. I wrote six chapters of the novel and then stopped. . . ."[16]

In 1904, after Tseng P'u and his friends had founded the Forest of Fiction Book Company, Ting Tsu-yin (1871–1930), Hsü Nien-tz'u (1875–1908), and Tseng P'u went to discuss the novel with Chin Sung-ts'en. Tseng P'u expressed a desire to continue it since Chin himself did not like the work. After an agreement was reached, Tseng P'u kept the first two chapters more or less intact, and together with Chin worked out the plan for a sixty-chapter novel. Even the chapter headings were decided upon.

Chin's original conception of the novel can be seen in an advertisement printed in 1904 before the manuscript was turned over to Tseng P'u:

This book tells about the life of Sai-chin-hua; its contents include Sino-Russian relations, the Pamir Agreement, the Russian nihilists, the Manchurian Incident, recent revolutionary activity in Shanghai, the Tokyo Braves, the Kwangsi incident, Sino-Japanese diplomatic relations, and Russia's reoccupation of Manchuria. It also includes innumerable historical incidents, new schools of thought, strange happenings, and anecdotes all excitingly told and fascinating. . . .[17]

It was defined as a "political novel" (*cheng-chih hsiao-shuo*). Tseng P'u's advertisement in 1905 read:

This book uses the famous courtesan Sai-chin-hua as the protagonist to tell the history of the past thirty years, including the conflict between the new and the old, the period of old learning, the Sino-Japanese War, and the reform movement. All the incidents and anecdotes are realistically told. An unprecedented masterpiece in the world of fiction.[18]

Both writers, so it appears from their advertisements, wanted to exploit the name of Sai-chin-hua even though Tseng P'u had expressed reservations about Chin's use of her. He believed that Chin had put too much emphasis on her, thus making *Flower* like K'ung Shang-jen's (1648–1718) play *T'ao-hua shan* (*The Peach Blossom Fan*), or Han Tzu-yüan's (1856–1894) *Hai-shang hua lieh-chuan* (The Lives of Shanghai Flowers). The first is an early Ch'ing drama about the downfall of the Ming dynasty in 1644, with a love affair between a patriotic young scholar and a courtesan of great beauty and character as the core of the work.[19] The latter is a famous novel about the lives of singing-girls in Shanghai. Tseng P'u merely wanted to use Sai-chin-hua as the connecting thread with which to link together the many historical incidents and anecdotes of this period of change.

After Tseng P'u took over the task of continuing the novel, he worked steadily on it for three months, and completed twenty chapters at one stretch. It was published in two volumes of ten chapters each.

According to Tseng Hsü-pai, the author's eldest son, when his father worked on the novel, he had collected stacks of clippings and notes on the period and on the personalities about whom he wrote. These clippings and notes, unfortunately, were all left behind in Shanghai when Tseng left for Taiwan, so that we are unable to see the raw materials from which Tseng P'u fashioned his novel.[20]

Tseng P'u never completed the sixty-chapter version. The twenty chapters that he wrote in 1904 formed the core of *Flower* although five more chapters were printed serially in the *Forest of Fiction* magazine in 1907; eventually it was revised, expanded, and continued to thirty-five chapters in the late 1920s.[21] But the most substantial and enduring part of the novel is the first twenty-four chapters. My evaluation of *Flower* will be based on this unrevised twenty-four chapter edition published in 1916.[22] In my opinion, this edition embodies the spirit and letter of the late Ch'ing period. The revised version was written at a different time when the circumstances were radically changed and therefore reflects other interests.

III   *An Evaluation of* Flower

What were the reasons for *Flower*'s popularity when it was first published? First, the novel dealt with a subject of perennial interest to the Chinese audience: the romance between a talented scholar and a beautiful courtesan *(ts'ai-tzu chia-jen)*. Moreover, the talented scholar and beautiful courtesan were based on actual people whom the reader could easily identify. Chin Wen-ch'ing, the hero, was in real life Hung Chün (1840–1893), "the number one scholar on the golden register of scholars" *(chin-pang chuang-yüan)*. Fu Ts'ai-yün, the beautiful singing-girl, was in real life the famous courtesan Sai-chin-hua (1874–1936), "the number one beauty on the register of beauties" *(hua-pang chuang-yüan)*. Second, with these two colorful personalities as the hero and heroine, Tseng P'u wove into the narrative many anecdotes about prominent scholar-officials of the time, such as Weng T'ung-ho, P'an Tsu-yin, Li Tz'u-ming, Li Hung-chang, Chang Chih-tung, Wu Ta-ch'eng, and Chang P'ei-lun. The novel was a roman à clef that appealed to the more traditional Chinese readers. Third, it expressed strong anti-Manchu sentiments. It praised the activities of the secret societies and revolutionaries, and condemned the examination system and many traditional social conventions. It expressed the mood of unrest and discontent of the time. Fourth, the novel fascinated its readers with descriptions of Berlin and St. Petersburg, and with the heretical ideologies of Saint-Simon and the Russian nihilists. Finally, the novel would not have been successful had it not been for the sensitive portrayal of character, and the interplay of satire, comedy, and condemnation.

The severest critic of *Flower* after Hu Shih must be Jaroslav Průšek, who wrote in 1970: "The way Tseng P'u linked the individual story of his heroes with historical facts, however, is a perfect example of how the mechanical combination of heterogeneous material ends in artistic fiasco. . . . The author revealed stylistic skill and showed that he had learned some of the European techniques by which to express the mental state of his heroes. Unfortunately his attempt to insert into this unified and romantically conceived narrative incident showing the struggle of different nations for freedom was an, utter failure. All these episodes remain alien elements artificially tacked on to the main plot. . . . In the mind of the author the unifying element was probably his admiration for heroes of all kinds, but he did not manage to find adequate literary expression for his admiration." [23]

Any serious attempt to evaluate *Flower* must answer this charge. In his essay Průšek examines five late Ch'ing novels, *Kuan-ch'ang hsien-hsing chi* (The Bureaucracy Exposed), *Er-shih nien mu-tu chih kuai hsien-chuang* (*Vignettes of The Late Ch'ing*), *Chiu ming ch'i yüan* (Nine Murders), *Lao-Ts'an yu chi* (*The Travels of Lao Ts'an*) and *Nieh-hai hua* (Flower) to show that, from the point of view of the function of the narrator, there were no new literary departures from the "traditional form of the storyteller's narration." Even though the late Ch'ing writers felt that the old literary forms were inadequate, they were not powerful enough to break free from the traditional mold. Consequently, Průšek finds all the above-mentioned novels deficient, except for *Travels* which he believed reveals a unified conception because of its "subjective atmosphere" and "unity of mood." The other novels are disjointed, artificial and episodic.

Průšek surmises that Tseng P'u's "admiration for heroes of all kinds" may be the underlying unifying principle for *Flower*. This is an inadequate explanation, since it is not with admiration that Tseng P'u described all of his characters nor is this truly the underlying principle. Let us consider that in *Flower*, aside from the main line of action of the protagonists, Chin Wen-ching and his concubine Fu Ts'ai-yün, there are fourteen self-contained episodes or anecdotes.[24] Now, are there any other meaningful relationships, or a "semantic organization," which underlie these anecdotes other than a mere mechanical combination of elements? Yes, a unifying principle is found in the fact that practically all of the anecdotes are about a dozen or so high-level officials or men of letters in Peking: the late Ch'ing intelligentsia. They form an elite coterie who know each other and work together. Unlike *The Bureaucracy Exposed* or *Vignettes* whose characters exist in self-contained episodes and never meet and interact, the characters in *Flower* often get together on occasions, such as for discussions of world affairs, banquets, birthday celebrations, or simple casual meetings. Furthermore, these anecdotes tell about aspects of their private lives, for example, the opportunistic Chuang Lun-ch'iao's rise in the "Purification clique" (*Ch'ing-liu tang*) and his downfall, the venerable P'an Pa-ying's promotion of Kung-yang learning, Chuang Shou-hsiang's flirtations with his housekeeper, the wealthy Yü Yang-po's attempts to buy office, or the Manchu nobleman Chu Pao-t'ing's romance with a flowerboat girl.

Tseng P'u wrote about the late Ch'ing intelligentsia, and his novel reflects the outlook of this milieu. The older members of this elite, like Li Ch'un-k'o and P'an Pa-ying, when confronted with the rapidly changing late Ch'ing world, hold on to the past with great tenacity and indulge themselves in the traditional pleasures. Members of the middle generation, like Chin Wen-ch'ing, Lu Feng-ju, and Ho Chüeh-chai, try to modernize themselves by learning about foreign affairs. But their efforts prove to be superficial and ineffective, even destructive. Their traditional outlook cannot really be changed. The younger generation, like Wen Yün-kao, Chiang Chien-yun, Sun Yat-sen, and Shih Chien-ju, turn to reform or revolution. The old-style literati are candidly described in the birthday party for Li Ch'un-k'o. The concerns of the modernizers are hotly debated at the banquet at Wei-ch'un yüan. And the activities of the revolutionaries are portrayed at their secret meeting in Canton.

On close examination, these anecdotes, principally, show the degeneration of the ruling elite: their weakness for sensual pleasures, their passion for antiquated studies, their esoteric interests, and their pedantic scholarship. In short, Tseng P'u's *Flower* is a novel about the decline of the late Ch'ing intelligentsia written by a member of that class with the interests of the educated readers of that period in mind. There was no need for Tseng P'u to condemn or praise any group outright; the circumstances of the time were clear enough for the reader to form his own opinion.

With regard to the revolutionaries and, by association, the Russian nihilists, they were both of great concern not only to late Ch'ing intellectuals but also the late Ch'ing novelists. Both Tseng P'u and Liu E, the author of *Travels*, wrote about them. Comparing them with the Boxers, Liu E was more fearful of the revolutionaries because of their denial of the existence of spirits: "if there are no spirits, then you don't need to respect your ancestors. . . .If you say there are no spirits, then there is no retribution from Hell, and no punishment from Heaven, and you can act in any way, defying Heaven's laws, and arouse the unholy joy of dissolute youths. . . they will practice their tricks against morality." [25] Liu E, also a member of the educated (but unorthodox) elite, expressed a most conservative view with regard to the revolutionaries, but condoned, in his novel, the traditional pleasures of poetry, wine, opium-smoking, and concubinage.

Tseng P'u, by contrast, viewed the revolution as a much-needed "peal of thunder which will awaken the Chinese from their two-hundred-year-old illusory dream and sweep away the hundreds of thousands of foul-smelling barbarians. Stand on the rooftops, and let us yell out and all our shackles will be broken. There is no question that we will become the leader in all of Asia!" [26] It cannot be denied that Tseng P'u was carried away by his enthusiasm, or that he dramatized and romanticized his description of the revolutionaries (and misplaced them chronologically) and the Russian nihilists, but both groups were very much on the mind of the late Ch'ing intelligentsia.

The fate of China at the end of the century is another crucial unifying factor which must be taken into consideration in evaluating *Flower*. The decline of China at the end of the century is intertwined with and inseparable from the fate of the main protagonist Chin Wen-ch'ing, as the fate of the protagonist is inseparable from his tragic but romantic involvement with the heroine Fu Ts'ai-yün. But this beauty-scholar romance is based on the theme of retribution rather than romantic love and therefore doomed to a tragic end. The whole of *Flower* is the fate of Chin Wen-ch'ing written large, and symbolically linked to the fate of China in the late nineteenth century. Understood from this perspective, *Flower* is a powerful and coherent expression of the concerns of the late Ch'ing intelligentsia written in the elegant and objective manner of *The Scholars*; it leaves the matter of ultimate judgment up to the thoughtful, educated reader. And it is Tseng P'u's ties to the past that make *Flower* on one hand ambivalent and controversial and on the other attractive and unforgettable.

CHAPTER 6

A Writer, Publisher, and Translator

AFTER its publication, *Flower* was widely read, but its author, Tseng P'u, remained relatively obscure for a time because he used the pen name The Sick Man of East Asia (*Tung-ya ping fu*). But Tseng P'u was not inactive. He was instrumental in founding the Forest of Fiction Book Company (*Hsiao-shuo lin shu-she*), which specialized in printing novels, both originals written in Chinese and translated ones. He also contributed poetry, translations, and fiction to the *Forest of Fiction* magazine which was published from 1907 to 1908 by the same company.

I *Tseng P'u and Forest of Fiction Book Company*

Tseng P'u had a long and abiding interest in literature, but it was not until his serious illness from 1900 to 1903, caused by overwork, that his interest turned to fiction in particular, or that he realized the importance of fiction in the field of literature as a whole. In 1904, after his recovery, Tseng P'u—together with several friends from his home town of Ch'ang-shu, Hsü Nien-tz'u, Ting Tsu-yin, and Chu Yüan-sheng—founded the Forest of Fiction Book Company. He was the general manager and Hsü Nien-tz'u the general editor. The company was to be devoted solely to the publication of works of fiction. Tseng P'u's avowed purpose for founding the company was to fight the longstanding prejudice against fiction by publishing both new Chinese novels and translations of Western and Japanese literature.[1]

In China, "fiction" (*hsiao-shuo*—originally meaning "chit-chat of no great importance") had been generally regarded as inconsequential writings undeserving of serious study. There were many reasons for this disparaging view. Fiction was a late-comer on the Chinese literary scene; it did not achieve a fully recognizable form until the early fourteenth century, thus lagging behind the development of poetry by two thousand years. Written in a form of the vernacular, the spoken language of the common man, Chinese fiction hardly equalled the exalted dignity of poetry written in the classical, literary language of the educated elite. Compared with historical and philosophical writings, fiction fared even worse. "Fiction is at once opposed to official historiography for its lack of concern with truth, and to serious, improving literature for its frivolous, salacious, and often politically subversive character. Even though a few exceptional works like *Shui-hu* (*The Water Margin*) and *Hung-lou* (*The Dream of the Red Chamber*) have attracted, in the course of time, a large body of affirmative criticism and commentary, prefaces to most novels are apologetic or defensive in tone. These prefaces readily concede the low breeding of fiction but emphasize its educational impact on the intended audience, who cannot be expected to read or understand the more serious kind of literature." [2] The "low breeding of fiction"— which refers to the humble origins of fiction by the street-corner story-teller—and the supposedly illiterate audience of fiction were also stigmas difficult to overcome. Although the effect of fiction has long been recognized, as a literary genre and as an instrument of social reform, Chinese fiction had to wait until the literary revolution of the twentieth century before it was to find its rightful place.

In the late nineteenth century, before Tseng P'u had made his decision to publish, there were already the beginnings of a "revolution" in the late Ch'ing world of fiction. Yen Fu (1854–1921) and Hsia Tseng-yu (1861–1924) had launched a reevaluation of fiction in their long and learned essay "Announcing Our Policy to Print a Supplementary Fiction Section." [3] They recognized the power of fiction to influence and used biological and Darwinian arguments to support their position. However, their conclusion was that Chinese fiction had so far exerted only an evil influence because its readers were not learned enough to decipher hidden meanings: ". . . when the ancients made fiction, each had in mind a subtle and refined purpose that, however, is conveyed beyond words and is too deeply hidden to be fathomable. And because people of shallow learning are addicted to fiction, the world has suffered incalculably from the poison of fiction and it is difficult to speak of its benefits." [4] Therefore, in order to achieve the desired results, a new fiction must be created with its intents and purposes clearly spelled out.

In 1902, Liang Ch'i-ch'ao, the most forceful, eloquent, and influential spokesman for this new movement, wrote his famous and often-quoted essay "On the Relationship between Fiction and Public Order." [5] In this essay Liang went a step further than Yen Fu by isolating and identifying the four essential factors that account for the powerful influence of fiction. The power of fiction, according to

Liang, is produced by the conjunction of four elements or processes: immersion (*hsün*), permeation (*ch'in*), stimulation (*tz'u*), and elevation (*t'i*). The first two elements are slow, unconscious processes which gradually affect the reader. The first, immersion, is concerned with the spatial aspect where the reader is bathed in the "vapors" of the story, as it were; the second, permeation, is concerned with the temporal dimension, the penetration of the vapors into the mind of the reader over a period of time. These two gradual processes are complemented by the third, stimulation, which is a sudden awakening or coming to awareness. Finally, the fourth element, elevation, acts on the individual from within to make the reader identify with the hero or heroine of the story.

After explaining these four processes, Liang goes on to say that powerful as these forces of fiction may be, they can be made to serve either good or evil: "How good is fiction! And how frightening is fiction!" Similar to Yen Fu, Liang argues that, so far, Chinese fiction has served only an evil function. In fact, the Chinese people's superstitions, their greediness for rank and wealth, their penchant for corruption, intrigue, and opportunism, their irresponsibility and licentiousness, and their lawless rebelliousness are all attributed to traditional Chinese fiction. And because of its powerful and widespread influence, he argues that if we want to renovate the people, we must begin by renovating fiction. With powerful rhetoric, Liang writes:

> If we wish to renovate the people of a nation, we must first renovate the fiction of that nation. Therefore, if we wish to renovate their sense of morality, we must renovate fiction; if we wish to renovate their religion, we must renovate fiction; if we wish to renovate their political system, we must renovate fiction; if we wish to renovate their customs and habits, we must renovate fiction; if we wish to renovate their learning and arts, we must renovate fiction; even if we wish to renovate their mind and morality, we must renovate fiction! [6]

It was this essay that sounded the clarion call of a literary revolution in the late Ch'ing world of fiction.

Tseng P'u, undoubtedly, was influenced by Liang Ch'i-ch'ao. On the other hand, he may have arrived at his own realization of the importance of fiction by reading and studying French literature.

When Tseng P'u and his friends founded the Forest of Fiction Book Company in 1904, several other companies were already printing works of fiction. The largest was Commercial Press which published

193 titles of fiction during the late Ch'ing period; next was Forest of Fiction Company with 116 titles; third, Reformed Fiction Company (*Kai-liang hsiao-shuo she*) with eighty-one titles; and fourth, Wisdom Company (*Kuang-chih shu-chü*) with thirty-nine titles. These figures are based on A Ying's survey of 462 original and 633 translated works of fiction published during the late Ch'ing period.[7] Although Tseng P'u's avowed purpose was to introduce systematically great works of Western literature to China, the financial realities of marketing and disagreement on policy among the joint-owners forced the Forest of Fiction Company to publish a large number of popular adventure stories and detective stories, featuring such characters as Sherlock Holmes, Nick Carter, and Martin Hewitt. But financially the company was successful.

After its first year of operation, Forest of Fiction moved to Tunghua district on Soochow Road, a location popularly known as Ch'ip'an Street (Chessboard Street), the heart of the bookselling district in Shanghai where bookstores and stationery shops were all located on one block. For the first year, printing for the company was done in Japan. In 1905 the company bought its own printing facilities in Fu-hai district on Park Road: the East Asia Printing Company (*Tungya yin-shu kuan*) formerly owned by Tseng P'u's brother-in-law Wu Szu-ch'ien. For the next few years, Forest of Fiction published numerous works, reaching its peak year in 1907 with thirty-eight titles.

Also in 1907, at a stockholders' meeting, Hsü Nien-tz'u suggested that a subsidiary company be established to publish reference works, and a stationery store to sell school supplies and children's toys. Against Tseng P'u's objections, the stockholders approved Hsü's plan for expansion. Consequently, Hung-wen kuan was founded to compile and publish reference books, and Mei-shu kuan was founded to sell school supplies and children's toys. A large sum of money was invested in compiling big, thick volumes of reference works. Twenty-four volumes were planned, on such subjects as botany, mining, mathematics, chemistry. Unfortunately, these volumes did not have a market at the time. Because of insolvency, the entire complex collapsed in 1908. The idea of an interconnected system of stores was good, but it was ahead of the needs of the time.

During the five years of its operation from 1904 to 1908, Forest of Fiction did make a significant contribution to the late Ch'ing literary world. It ranked second to Commercial Press, the largest publishing concern of the time, in publishing literature. Of course, Forest of

Fiction could not compare with Commercial Press's overall publication program which included many textbooks. Of Commercial Press's 193 titles in literature, only eleven were original works of fiction; the rest were translations. Of Forest of Fiction's 116 titles, seventeen were original works, and the rest translations. It can be seen that translations were the mainstay of the publishing trade during this period.

Tseng P'u was the general manager of Forest of Fiction Company. He probably played an important part in founding and financing the company, but left the daily operations to his colleagues, such as Hsü Nien-tz'u, Ting Tsu-yin, Huang Mo-hsi, and others who were deeply involved in the literary movement at the time. There is little record of Tseng P'u's activities during this time; we only catch glimpses of him here and there. For instance, in the later part of 1904, he spent a three-month period completing twenty chapters of his *Flower*; probably in 1907, he made a special trip to Peking to see Lin Shu and discuss with him a systematic program for translating Western literature which Lin Shu rejected. He translated part of Alexandre Dumas's *La Reine Margôt* in 1908. Toward the end of this period, he was drawn more and more into politics, both by force of circumstances, on the one hand, and by his feeling of literary isolation on the other.

II *Tseng P'u and the* Forest of Fiction *Magazine*

In February, 1907, the Forest of Fiction Book Company began publication of a literary magazine called *Forest of Fiction*. Tseng P'u was one of its principal contributors. Chapters XXI to XXV of his novel *Flower*, some of his classical poetry, a biographical sketch of Alexandre Dumas *père*, and a partial translation of Dumas's *La Reine Margôt* were published in its pages.

Although Tseng P'u was not the editor of *Forest of Fiction*, he must have played a significant part in determining its policy. Twelve issues were published from 1907 to 1908, and it became one of the four best known and one of the most important literary magazines of the late Ch'ing period. The others were *Hsin hsiao-shuo* (New Fiction), *Hsiu-hsiang hsiao-shuo* (Illustrated Fiction), and *Yüeh-yüeh hsiao-shuo* (The All-Story Monthly). Practically all of the important novels of the late Ch'ing period were first serialized in these magazines.

New Fiction was founded by Liang Ch'i-ch'ao in 1903.[8] Its first issue carried Liang's important essay "On the Relationship between

Fiction and Public Order" which marked the beginning of a new era
in fiction. Under the editorship of Liang Ch'i-ch'ao, the magazine
published twenty-four issues. Aside from fiction (its most important
contribution), it also published drama, translations, fiction criticism,
essays, and poetry. Its publication of fiction included Liang's own
unfinished "political novel" *Hsin Chung-kuo wei lai chi* (The Future
of New China); Wu Wo-yao's historical novel *T'ung-shih* (A History of
Pain), his satirical novel *Erh-shih nien mu-tu chih kuai hsien-chuang
(Vignettes from the Late Ching),* his detective novel *Chiu ming ch'i
yüan* (The Strange Case of Nine Murders), and many stories by other
writers. In retrospect, we must conclude that *New Fiction* did fulfill
its function of eliciting a new view of fiction and stimulated much
interest in creating a literature with a serious sense of social commitment.

Illustrated Fiction, under the editorship of Li Pao-chia, published
seventy-two issues from 1903 to 1906.[9] Its avowed purpose was
similar to Liang Ch'i-ch'ao's *New Fiction*. It also published drama,
poetry, translations, in addition to fiction and fiction criticism. Li
Pao-chia's novels *Wen-ming hsiao-shih* (A Short History of Civilization), *Huo ti-yü* (Living Hell), and Liu E's *Lao Ts'an yu-chi (The
Travels of Lao Ts'an)* appeared first in its pages. *Illustrated Fiction*
had a broader, more popular appeal than *New Fiction* and was
directed more toward exposing the evils of the day.

The All-Story Monthly, under the editorship of Wu Wo-yao, Chou
Kuei-sheng, and others, published twenty-four issues from 1906 to
1908.[10] It was essentially a continuation of *Illustrated Fiction* with a
change of editorship after the death of Li Pao-chia in 1906. It serialized five of Wu Wo-yao's novels. Two of the most outstanding ones
were *Liang Chin yen-i* (Romance of the Two Chin Dynasties) and
Chieh-yü hui (Ashes of Death). The most innovative feature of the
magazine was the publication of the new short story form, an ex-
perimental genre of the time.

Forest of Fiction, under the editorship of Huang Mo-hsi, was the
latest of the four magazines. Twelve issues were published from 1907
to 1908. Although its format resembled the other four magazines, its
critical stance differed significantly from its predecessors. The first
issue contained two important essays. The first, entitled "The Opening Editorial Statement of *Forest of Fiction*" (Hsiao-shuo lin *fa-k'an
tz'u*), was by the editor Huang Mo-hsi.[11] The second, entitled "The
Reasons for the Founding of *Forest of Fiction*" (Hsiao-shuo lin *yüan-
ch'i*), was by a frequent contributor, Hsü Nien-tz'u.[12] The views

expressed in these essays broke new ground in Chinese literary criticism and differed significantly from Liang Ch'i-ch'ao's views expressed in 1903. In that essay, Liang condemned traditional fiction, called for the creation of a new fiction to renovate the people, and stressed only the social function of literature with no mention at all of any aesthetic criteria for evaluating literature in itself.

In *Forest of Fiction*, there was a clear turning away from this attitude. Hsü Nien-tz'u introduced the philosophies of Georg Wilhelm Friedrich Hegel and Julius Hermann von Kirchmann to reevaluate Chinese literature; and Huang Mo-hsi warned against attaching too much importance to a work of fiction, as compared to the time when too little attention was given to the genre. Commenting on the attitudes of his contemporaries, Huang wrote:

As soon as a work of fiction is published, it is credited with improving the nation; when a work is evaluated, it is praised for its effectiveness in reforming the manners and morals of the people. Everyone hails it and studies it. . . . Even though the work may be crude, insignificant, and not worthy of praise, it is introduced as if it were the laws of a nation, the scriptures of a religion, a textbook for schools, and a model for the state and society. How can this be the case? [13]

He then suggested that fiction was a branch of literature which sought beauty and that the proper function of fiction was not moral instruction. He concluded: "Forest of Fiction Company is publishing *Forest of Fiction* magazine simply because fiction is fiction. Moral instruction is the affair of Hung-wen kuan [which publishes textbooks] and not that of our *Forest of Fiction.*" [14]

Hsü Nien-tz'u's approach to fiction is on a higher level of sophistication than Liang Ch'i-ch'ao's. Borrowing from the Hegelian and Kirchmann's philosophy of art, Hsü arrives at his own syncretic view of literature: first, the end of art is rational unification with nature; second, beauty lies in the realization of the concrete rather than remaining in the abstract; third, pleasure derived from beauty is based on the presentation of reality; fourth, the essence of beauty is based on the imitation of reality; and fifth, a special characteristic of beauty is its imaginative quality. On the basis of these five criteria, Hsü emphasizes the universality of Chinese fiction, and points out the superiority of Chinese fiction in certain respects vis-à-vis Western fiction. The Chinese novel, for example, often uses a large cast of characters and many lines of action. Whereas the Western novel more frequently focuses on the fate and development of one or two individuals. According to Hsü, a large cast of characters is more difficult to portray than a single character.[15]

These were the reactions of courageous and more sophisticated readers of Chinese fiction who were against the predominant utilitarian view of fiction held during the late Ch'ing period. They believed that fiction should not be judged on the basis of its social function alone but also according to aesthetic criteria.

The general format and contents of *Forest of Fiction* did not differ significantly from those of its three famous predecessors. There was the usual selection of "social novels" (*she-hui hsiao-shuo*), "scientific novels" (*k'o-hsüeh hsiao-shuo*), "detective stories" (*chen-t'an hsiao-shuo*), "romances" (*hsieh-ch'ing hsiao-shuo*), "military novels" (*chün-shih hsiao-shuo*), "historical novels" (*li-shih hsiao-shuo*), and other miscellaneous ones. *Forest of Fiction* did have a special column called "Report on New Books," which briefly described recently published books, including those not published by Forest of Fiction Company. Also in the ninth issue of *Forest of Fiction*, Hsü Nien-tz'u printed a survey of all works of fiction published in 1907; these amounted to over a hundred titles. Out of a total of 108 titles, forty-one were published by Forest of Fiction Company, forty-four by Commercial Press. The rest were published by other smaller companies.[16] Another interesting feature was a special section devoted to the works of and about Ch'iu Chin (1882–1907), the famous woman martyr who was summarily executed on July 15, 1907, for her revolutionary activities. At the risk of government censure *Forest of Fiction* published her works. *Forest of Fiction* continued its sporadic publication until November, 1908. By this time the era of the late-Ch'ing political novel had come to an end. A new type of "mandarin duck and butterfly" (*yüan-yang hu-tieh p'ai*) novels with their tales of love and romance came to dominate the literary scene.

Tseng P'u himself had also by this time begun to move away from literature into politics. Tseng Hsü-pai tells us that his father played a part in the Association to Prepare for Establishment of a Constitutional Government (*Yü-pei li-hsien kung-hui*) established on December 16, 1906. He was involved in the disputes over financing and management of the Shanghai-Hangchow-Ningpo Railway. Finally, his participation in demonstrations against the appointment of Chang Tseng-yang (1843–1921) as governor of Kiangsu led to a warrant for his arrest by the Ch'ing government. Chang was the official responsible for being excessively brutal in handling the Ch'iu Chin affair and now he was being assigned to Kiangsu. In order to escape arrest, Tseng P'u joined the advisory group of the relatively enlightened Manchu governor-general of Kiangsu and Chekiang, Tuan-fang, one of the five progressive officials who had been sent abroad in 1905–1906 to learn about constitutional government in foreign countries. This seemingly anti-revolutionary move marked the end of Tseng P'u's early literary career, and the beginning of a political career which was to last almost twenty years. He said that his participation in politics was forced upon him by the circumstances: "Speaking about my being an official, that's a joke! Do you think that it was my ambition to be an official? It was just a few monkey tricks which I was forced to play. These few bitter pages in the history of my life, forgive me if I do not go into them here." [17]

III   *The Political Interregnum*

Although politics was not to his liking, Tseng P'u proved himself to be a capable administrator. He was low-keyed, scholarly, and conscientious. He did not speak unless the occasion called for it, and when he did speak, his opinion was listened to. Tseng P'u held the position of expectant prefect (*hou-pu chih-fu*, one of many advisory offices) of Chekiang province before the Revolution of 1911. After the revolution broke out, Tseng P'u relinquished his post and returned to Shanghai. In 1912, he was approached by a friend, Yang I-chih, to run for a seat in the Kiangsu provincial assembly. He was elected, and in the winter of 1912 his political career in Kiangsu provincial politics began.

While in the assembly, he was the chairman of several committees, including one on finance. In the spring of 1914, he was selected by the assembly to go to Peking as the Kiangsu representative to attend the national meeting of financial officers from all the provinces (*ch'üan-kuo ko-sheng ts'ai-cheng hui-i*) called by Yüan Shih-k'ai, who was the first president of the young republic. At this meeting, Tseng P'u lashed out fearlessly at Feng Kuo-chang (1859–1919), the military governor of Kiangsu from December 11, 1913, to June 30, 1914, who had stationed his troops in Kiangsu and caused undue hardships for the people. It was said that even Yüan Shih-k'ai visibly changed color at Tseng P'u's remarks. [18] After a brief stay in Peking, Tseng P'u returned to Kiangsu. In 1914 he was placed in charge of the Bureau of Official Enterprises (*kuan-ch'an ch'u*), a post he held from 1914 to 1921. This office had the dual function of overseeing government-owned enterprises and the rich delta lands along the lower Yangtze

River. Tseng P'u had a hand in establishing this office because he saw the necessity of carefully safeguarding these basic resources of Kiangsu so that they would not become prey to the greedy military governors.

While holding this office, he was instrumental in Kiangsu's movement to oppose Yüan Shih-k'ai's monarchical ambitions. Tseng P'u contributed personal funds to subsidize the troops of Kiangsu.[19] In the winter of 1916, after the death of Yüan Shih-k'ai, Tseng P'u was summoned by President Li Yüan-hung (1864–1928) to take on duties concerning land reclamation and development in northern Anhwei province.

Although Tseng P'u was actively engaged in politics from 1912 to 1921, he still had time to pursue his interest in French literature. In October, 1913, Yu-cheng Book Company published his translation of Victor Hugo's *Quatre-vingt Trieze*; in 1914, *Monthly Fiction* published his translation of Hugo's *Angelo, Tyran de Padoue*; and in 1916, Yu-cheng Book Company published his translation of Hugo's *Lucrèce Borgia*. When Tseng Yao-chung, Tseng P'u's second son, went to study in Germany in 1919, he purchased at his father's request large quantities of books on French literature. These books inspired Tseng P'u to write a history of French literature. He worked industriously, studying, writing, and translating. Unfortunately, he overexerted himself again and showed signs of heart trouble. Another unhappy incident that occurred about this time was the death of his only daughter, Te, in August, 1918. Heartbroken and in ill-health, Tseng P'u resigned from his post as head of the Bureau of Official Enterprises and assumed the sinecure of rice regulation.

Until now, the prosperous provinces of Kiangsu and Chekiang had been spared the havoc of war between the various militarists. Beginning in 1923, however, even these provinces were drawn into the conflict as the Fengtien and Chihli cliques in the north began to extend their powers southward into the Yangtze valley. It was during this period that Tseng P'u assumed the highest office of his political career. He became Secretary of the Treasury in 1924 and Secretary of Administrative Affairs in 1926.[20]

Tseng P'u was appointed the Secretary of the Treasury by Han Kuo-chün, the civilian governor of Kiangsu, probably in December, 1924. As the Secretary of the Treasury, Tseng P'u had to deal with Chang Tsung-ch'ang (1881–1932) who belonged to the Fengtien clique, and Ch'i Hsieh-yüan (1897–1946), the former military governor of Kiangsu who belonged to the rival Chihli clique. Chang was leading a large force to attack Ch'i in the Shanghai region. At the request of the Shanghai Merchants Association and other groups, Tseng P'u was appointed to persuade Ch'i and Chang not to fight in this area; but he did not succeed. As Chang made his way to Shanghai along the Nanking-Shanghai railway, he defeated Ch'i's forces. After Ch'i fled to Japan, Tseng P'u had to deal with Chang's demands. But he considered his most important function to protect Kiangsu. While he was in office, he paid special attention to education and founded an agency for appropriating educational funds for the province—an important achievement in those chaotic times. Tseng P'u and Han Kuo-chün were both relieved of their posts after the new military governor, Lu Yung-hsiang (1867–1930) was installed. They had held office for about four months.

Tseng P'u's second term of high office was under Sun Ch'üan-fang, a Chihli man who proclaimed himself Commander-in-Chief of the Allied Armies of Five Provinces: Chekiang, Kiangsu, Anhwei, Fukien, and Kiangsi (*wu-sheng lu-chün tsung-ssu-ling*) on October 15, 1925. After consolidating his position over the five provinces, Sun summoned Ch'en T'ai-i and Tseng P'u to serve as the provincial governor and secretary of administrative affairs, respectively. These two men took office on the condition that Sun Ch'üan-fang would not interfere in the internal affairs of the province. After nine months' tenure, from December, 1925, to September, 1926, Tseng P'u resigned since Sun Ch'üan-fang refused to observe the conditions to which they had agreed. Ch'en T'ao-i held office a few months longer, and his resignation was announced on December 6, 1926.

Why did Tseng P'u remain in politics for so long? Many new developments in literature following the Literary Revolution of the late teens would have drawn away a man much less devoted to literature than Tseng P'u. Perhaps he wanted to fulfill the traditional role of the scholar-official, the goal he had not been able to achieve in late Ch'ing times. On the other hand, although outwardly Tseng P'u was in politics, privately he was engaged in literary work. He was preparing for his reemergence on the literary scene.

Once a friend asked Tseng P'u what his principle was in dealing with the avaricious militarists. He replied, "Under the circumstances, all I can do is to protect our province from the government. What more can I do?" [21] Unlike many unscrupulous officials who took advantage of these chaotic times to enrich themselves, Tseng P'u, after more than fifteen years of service, left office no richer than when he came. His friends gave accounts of his incorruptibility and uprightness while he was in office.

IV   Literature and Tseng's Quest for National Identity

In the years from 1908 to 1926, Tseng P'u had undergone a literary transformation. From his former role as a writer of traditional fiction, he emerged as a modern writer devoted to the frank pursuit of truth, beauty, and goodness. He incorporated these ideals into the name of his publishing company, Chen Mei Shan (Truth, Beauty, and Goodness), which he founded together with his eldest son, Tseng Hsü-pai, in 1927. The founding of this company marked the beginning of his second period of literary activity.

This was Tseng P'u's most prolific period. He translated several French plays, wrote an autobiographical novel, revised and continued his novel *Flower*; as magazine editor he replied to his readers, and wrote several studies of French authors. It was also a period in which he wrote frankly about himself, his ideals and ambitions, his disappointments and shortcomings, his views on literature and life. Whereas before he had been reticent, during this period he frequently revealed himself through his letters, his autobiographical novel, and his diary. He was much more personal in his writings than before. He discarded the earmarks of the traditional Chinese literati—classical prose and classical poetry. He wrote in the vernacular and constantly struggled with the problem of how to express himself honestly and frankly, how to be genuine and truthful.

Tseng P'u's autobiographical novel *Lu Nan-tzu* was, on the one hand, an aesthetic experience; on the other hand, it was his search for national identity. He examined the writings of his contemporaries who were influenced by Western literature, and was highly critical. He felt that there was too much imitation and not enough creativity and genuine expression of feeling—feelings and emotions which expressed China's national character. The term "national character," however, should not obscure for us the highly individualistic path that led Tseng P'u from his realistic novel of social criticism, *A Flower in An Ocean of Sin*, to his writings which explored the innermost recesses of the human heart.

As we have seen in Chapter 3, he tried to synthesize his concept of the Western romantic hero with that of the Chinese romantic hero; in other words, he was trying to strike a balance between the realistic and romantic tendencies. In the China of the 1920s, the Realists, led by Lu Hsün (1881–1936), took as their models Western writers such as Chekhov, Dostoevsky, and Balzac, whereas the Romantics, led by Kuo Mo-jo, took as their models Shelley, Goethe, and Nietzsche. Following Lu Hsün's example, the Realists exposed the harsh realities of society; they wrote about the sufferings of the common people, about their customs and beliefs that brought hardships upon themselves. The Romantics wrote about themselves, revealed their innermost thoughts and feelings—the grief, despair, and frustration of the individual. To show the highly complex and volatile nature of this period, when Kuo Mo-jo suddenly converted to Marxism in 1924, the motto of the Creationists changed from "art for art's sake" to "revolutionary literature." Aside from the two main trends of Realism and Romanticism, there were numerous side currents, such as the Crescent Moon Society which advocated "respectability" and "health" in literature, and another group that advocated "literature for nationalism." [22] This latter group included some of Tseng P'u's associates, such as Chu Ying-p'ing, Fu Yen-ch'ang, Shao Hsün-mei, and others. But Tseng P'u himself was not a member of any particular group.

Tseng P'u's literary motto during this later period was truth (*chen*), beauty (*mei*), and goodness (*shan*). For him, truth in literature meant genuineness and sincerity in feeling, no falsification or exaggeration. Beauty meant the effective use of words, sentences, and general expressions that would leave a lasting and pleasing impression in the mind of the reader. And goodness referred to the final end of literature that ought to be forward-looking, exploratory, and adventurous; it should point the way to goodness.[23] Tseng P'u cited these examples as contrary to his ideals:

Take the example of a fashionable Chinese gentleman dressed in a Western suit; obviously he can speak Chinese, but he persists in interjecting foreign expressions into his speech. This is certainly not being truthful (*chen*). Take the example of a secondhand shop that has lots of merchandise, but whose owner insists on displaying powders, rouges, and the tattered clothing of prostitutes, students, and disreputable women. This is certainly not being beautiful (*mei*). Finally, take a hospital whose function is to help people, and look after their general well-being; instead it poisons them, and on the pretext of healing them, extorts money from them. This is certainly not being good (*shan*).[24]

In other words the writer should not deceive but seek consistency, harmony, and truth. Confronted with the old and the new, the foreign and the native, the Chinese writer should try to blend them harmoniously together.

In his survey of the literary scene in the late 1920s, Tseng P'u was impressed by the progress made in various genres. There were new developments in poetry, in the essay, and in the short story. Of the many works, some were brilliant; but he was disappointed with the "unrestricted expression of personal feelings" which he felt was not genuine:

It cannot be denied that China's recent literary development has been brilliant. Unfortunately, the writers have been busily imitating Western models without realizing that they are forgetting about themselves. All the writings dealing explicitly with the subject of boy-meets-girl, needless to say, begin immediately with kissing and an arm around the girl's waist. Heroes commit suicide and fight duels at the slightest provocation. Young men in their despair are all like Werthers; in their heroic struggles they are like Jean-Christophes. But actually the Chinese are habitually restrained, and their nature is harmonious.

The *mal du siècle* of a scientifically undeveloped culture is its lack of sensitivity. It will "take Chang's hat and put it on Li's head," even though it does not fit. This is true especially in the use of language; the writers put aside accustomed Chinese word order, and use foreign word order. They call this Europeanization. If that is the case, then why not scrape off your yellow skin and make it white; pull out your black hair and grow blond hair; pluck out your eyes and put in blue ones; dismantle your skeleton and rearrange it; finally, why not just transplant your soul into the body of a foreigner. Then you will look much more like a Westerner.

I am in favor of reforming our literature. First we must express our national character and respect our own language. We must, within the framework of our own language, reform our literature so that it will embody our national character.[25]

As can be seen in the above, Tseng P'u was not so much concerned with the national crisis in politics, but with the crisis of national or cultural identity. He felt that the excessive show of emotion, impulsive action, and overdramatization were not in keeping with Chinese character which he regarded as restrained and harmonious. Tseng P'u attacked the emotional excesses of the early works of the Creation Society, such as Kuo Mo-Jo's first collection of poetry entitled *Nü-shen*, (The Goddess) and Yü Ta-fu's collection of short stories entitled *Ch'en-lun* (Sinking), and others. He argued that a nation or culture was like a human being who had his own personality and character. Literature was the expression of that character. The form and language of literature may change with time, but its essence remains fixed. That is the reason why English literature is English literature and not French literature, even if it is translated into French. To Tseng P'u then, the problem of the Chinese writer was how to remain faithful to the Chinese national character.

Even in his own diary Tseng P'u struggled with the problem of being frank and sincere. He wrote that he had kept diaries before but recorded only the weather, names of his visitors, and friends whom he visited. He never recorded anything that was from his heart. He attributed this to his use of the literary language and to the hypocrisy of Chinese culture. He pointed to the diaries of Weng T'ung-ho and Li Tz'u-ming; they were written only for posterity. Weng and Li recorded only their political activities and scholarly endeavors, but nothing about their personal lives. As for the literary language that he had used previously, Tseng P'u claimed that it was unsuited to the expression of personal feeling. In the diary that he began on May 22, 1928, Tseng P'u wrote down whatever came to his mind without regard to who might read it. He wanted to leave some genuine traces of his life to posterity:

I wanted to write without deliberate organization, without definite form. I will write whatever comes into my mind, in any fashion. But it will express my individuality. I will write whenever I can—about my thoughts and feelings. . . .[26]

In this spirit of frankness, Tseng P'u left us, in his diary, a brief but valuable account of his early love life and romance with his cousin Miss Ting, that should be read in conjunction with his autobiographical novel *Lu Nan-tzu*. We have only the fragment of his diary that he kept for four days from May 22 to May 25, 1928. The novel *Lu Nan-tzu*, written at about the same time, was the logical outgrowth of his principle of frankness and sincerity, his striving after beauty and harmony, and his quest for national identity.

Lu Nan-tzu was written over a two-year period (1927–1929). It progressed much more slowly and more leisurely than *Flower*, which took only three months to finish. The writing of this novel was like the retracing of his own life—the charting of his passage through the inner-environment of his seven basic emotions: joy, anger, sorrow, sensual pleasure, love, horror, and fear. At the same time, Tseng P'u struggled to find his cultural or national identity, and to arrive at a better understanding of himself.

In considering this novel in the context of Tseng P'u's personal life, we should keep three points in mind. First, Tseng P'u was writing a thinly disguised autobiographical novel—a "confessional" novel—in which he probed down to the bedrock of his emotions. It is a work of intense self-analysis which exposes his conflicts and ambivalences. It is profoundly different from *Flower*. Second, Tseng P'u was deeply concerned with frankness and sincerity in art, as well as in life. He did not want to falsify or exaggerate his feelings and emotions; he wanted to achieve consistency and harmony in his art. Third, he sought to express himself freely and yet remain consistent and in harmony with his ideal conception of what the national character was. As we have shown in Chapter 3, *Lu Nan-tzu* is the cumulative result of a variety of influences: French Romanticism, Zolaesque Naturalism, Buddhism, and the native Chinese literary tradition. Now the question is did Tseng P'u succeed in finding a national identity? This is difficult to answer since Chinese culture and the nation were in transition. But an answer is not really important. It was valuable insofar as he succeeded in finding his own identity. As Bruce Mazlish writes, "One of the main reasons for a person writing an autobiography is to discover, in the writing of it, what he has done; and thus what he is. What his life has meant and thus what it means in the present moment. . . ." [27]

V   *Translation and the Reform of Chinese Literature*

Translation had an important role to play in Tseng P'u's program to reform Chinese literature. As early as the turn of the century he realized the importance of translations of foreign literatures, not only as a source of amusement and profit, but also as part of a systematic program to bring Chinese literature into the arena of world literature. In 1907, Tseng P'u went to Peking to enlist the help of Lin Shu, the most prominent translator of Western fiction at the time, in carrying out a systematic program of translation of Western literature. He suggested, on that occasion, that representative works of various countries, of major historical periods, and of major schools of writing be selected for translation, rather than following a random selection process. Lin Shu, however, was not receptive to this proposal. Tseng P'u commented that Lin Shu's contribution to the development of Chinese literature would have been much greater had he made a systematic translation of major works of Western literature. Such a representative selection would have given Chinese writers a solid foundation upon which to develop their own new literature. As it was, many works of doubtful value were translated, but the important ones were left out. Lin translated twenty-five novels by Rider Haggard, five novels by Dickens, and several by Sir Walter Scott. Furthermore, Tseng P'u criticized Lin Shu for using literary Chinese in his translations instead of the vernacular. Use of the latter would have given those works a much wider audience, and it would have aided the development of the colloquial language itself. In both respects Lin Shu disappointed Tseng P'u.[28]

Translations and the study of Western literature were important for Tseng P'u because he believed in the theory of cross-fertilization of literary traditions. In the introductory editorial statement to the *Truth, Beauty, and Goodness* magazine, Tseng P'u wrote that if China wanted to reform her literature, then Chinese writers must learn as much about Western literary developments as possible, so that the "stale and rotten body" of the old literature could be replaced. With regard to Rabelais, Milton, Goethe, and Hugo, Tseng P'u wrote:

How could Rabelais have written *Gargantua and Pantagruel* if he had not known of Erasmus' *In Praise of Folly* and More's *Utopia*; . . . how could Milton have written *Paradise Lost* if he had not gone to Italy and been influenced by Dante; how could Goethe have written *Faust* if he had not lived in France and translated the *Roman de Renart*; and how could Hugo have created the French drama if he had not been exiled to England where he imbibed the spirit of Shakespeare's plays? It can be seen that no literature in the world can undergo significant change without stimulus from the outside. . . .[29]

To Tseng P'u, Chinese literature, similarly, could not change by itself, in isolation. It must have stimulus from outside. But he warned immediately, consistent with his views on national character, that foreign influences should merely stimulate creativity and not overwhelm it.

To a certain extent, the contemporary literary scene encouraged Tseng P'u. He believed that much had been accomplished in areas such as the informal essay, satirical pieces, psychological analysis, the short story, and poetry. However, he did not believe that any worthwhile major works of fiction, narrative poetry, criticism, or drama had been published. He concluded that although there were many fine works, they lacked "greatness." He attributed this defect to laziness and opportunism. He criticized the young writers of the time as being too clever. These writers, he continued, knew that writing articles, informal essays, and short stories brought them quick fame without much work; therefore, why should they trouble themselves with laborious translations or large-scale works which took up much precious time and with fewer rewards? But what was needed precisely at this time were translations of the best works of Western literature, which could be used as a foundation for China's own literary development. In the same way that the success of the European Renaissance had depended on translations of Greek and Roman works, the success of the new Chinese literature depended on translations of Western literature. Especially for those young writers who do not know a foreign language, this neglect was particularly harmful. Tseng P'u urged that if development of a new literature were to succeed, then young Chinese writers must overcome their laziness and opportunism and concentrate on translations. Tseng P'u made this proposal:

> The plan we have in mind is to make a careful survey of all the important works that have been translated into Chinese so far and compile a list. Whether or not the translations have been done well will be further discussed. Then make another list of important representative works from various periods, countries, and schools of writing which still need to be translated into Chinese. This list will be supplemented with notes and explanations and printed in our magazine for everyone to see and discuss. In this way we hope ultimately to set up a general goal for our translations.[30]

Although Tseng P'u spoke often about a systematic program of translation, he never did complete the list. His eldest son, Tseng Hsü-pai, made a survey of some translations from various European countries and from America;[31] and Chao Ching-shen (1902–   ) compiled another list of works translated from the Russian.[32] But the other part of the plan, the list of works that still needed to be translated, was never made. Tseng P'u's own translations did not amount to a systematic effort to translate the masterpieces of world literature, either. He devoted his attention to translating the plays of Victor Hugo, and some shorter works of various other nineteenth-century French writers, such as Zola, Balzac, Dumas *père*, etc. His more ambitious attempt to survey French literature from its very origins in Greek and Latin resulted in four essays published in the issues of the *Truth, Beauty, and Goodness* magazine.[33] Thus, his own efforts at laying a foundation for the reform of Chinese literature fell short of his goal.

Aside from translations, Tseng P'u's more comprehensive plan for the reform of Chinese literature was explained in his introductory editorial statement to *Truth, Beauty, and Goodness.* His general proposal had three parts. The first was that the colloquial language should be used for writing rather than the classical language. He argued that today was the day of the common man; therefore, the language of the common man should be used to write for the common man. Po Chü-i (772–846) should be taken as the example. Tradition has it that Po Chü-i, the great T'ang poet and statesman, would ask an illiterate old woman to listen to his poetry. If she understood it, he would be satisfied; if she did not understand it, he would make changes until she did. The second was that literature should reflect the characteristics of a nation or culture. Language, customs, and literary styles may change, but the basic characteristics of that nation remain the same, therefore the essence of that literature remains unchanged. For instance, English literature is not French literature, even though the former may be translated into French, and German literature is not Russian literature even though it may be translated into Russian; each has its own special characteristics. And the third part of Tseng's plan was that the ideal of art, in both form and content, was to achieve harmony and consistency. Whether the vernacular or the literary language was used, it should be used consistently throughout and not mixed.

From these basic assumptions, Tseng P'u formulated the following six general principles to guide the prospective writer:

1. Never interject literary language into dialogue.
2. Never use stock classical expressions in describing settings or emotions.
3. Do not imitate Japanese grammatical construction or pile on modifiers.
4. Do not use archaic vernacular expressions found in traditional fiction.
5. Do not use foreign letters to designate concealed names and places.
6. Only use interjections that are in common use.[34]

These three basic assumptions and six principles constituted Tseng P'u's concrete proposals for the reform of Chinese literature. To follow these assumptions and principles was easier said than done. Even Tseng P'u himself violated some of his own rules.

It is doubtful that Tseng P'u's literary program had much influence on his times. The vernacular movement, which began in 1917 with Hu Shih's essay "A Tentative Proposal for Literary Reform," was already well on its way before Tseng P'u made his proposal. Hu Shih's famous eight points for literary reform were:

1. Avoid the use of classical allusions.
2. Discard stale, time-worn literary phrases.
3. Discard the parallel construction of sentences.
4. Do not avoid using vernacular words and speech.
5. Follow literary grammar . . . .
6. Do not write that you are sick or sad when you do not feel sick or sad.
7. Do not imitate the writings of the ancients; what you write should reflect your own personality.
8. What you write should have meaning or real substance.[35]

These eight points were more comprehensive than Tseng P'u's six which were only refinements of the former. Ten years after Hu Shih's original proposal, although there was still sporadic opposition, the movement had won the day. It is true, however, as Tseng P'u pointed out, that some modern writers had already gone too far in imitating Western writers at the expense of slighting their own cultural heritage. Even Tseng P'u himself might be accused of this.

The major works of Tseng P'u's translation effort included five plays and a novel by Victor Hugo, a play by Molière, and two novellas of Zola. These works were chosen mainly as a stimulus to his own creative writing and not as part of his comprehensive program to translate the best works of Western literature. Tseng P'u was especially drawn to Victor Hugo because of cultural and subjective affinities. Chinese literary movements in the 1920s resembled the literary movements in France in the early eighteenth century. Both movements were reactions against the rigid "classicism" of the previous centuries. Literary revolutions were in the making, and Victor Hugo was the leader of the Romantic revolution in France. It is possible that Tseng P'u saw in himself the counterpart of Hugo in China. Even if Tseng P'u's larger effort to reform Chinese literature was not effective, his translation of Hugo's revolutionary plays into Chinese was significant. Furthermore, he has left us an interesting and valuable record of one writer's attempts.

CHAPTER 7

The End of a Literary Journey

AFTER more than twenty years, Tseng P'u once more turned to *Flower*. He revised, elaborated, and expanded it, bringing it to a total of thirty-five chapters. The events of the story were carried forward to the eve of the Hundred Days Reform Movement of 1898 from the time prior to the Sino-Japanese War of 1894 where the original version had stopped. The revised edition contains much material that detracts from the unity and coherence of the original twenty-four chapter version. For example, the original trio of scholars—Chin Wen-ch'ing, Ch'ien T'ang-ch'ing, and Ho Chüeh-chai— was enlarged to include Ts'ao Kung-fang (modelled on Tseng P'u's father) and thus form the "Four Friends" (*hai t'ien ssu yu*). The episode about Kung Hsiao-ch'i was expanded to include his father Kung Ting-an (Kung Tzu-chen [1792-1841]) who was believed to have had an affair with the famous Ch'ing poetess T'ai-ch'ing Hsi-lin-ch'un. The story about Chuang Lun-ch'iao was elaborated to include a Miao girl's recitation about the Black Flag's (a women's corps) battle against the French. These changes did nothing to enhance the art of this novel. The novel should have ended with Chapter XXIV after the death of Chin Wen-ch'ing, the protagonist, the only figure who can move the action of the story forward. Fu Ts'ai-yün cannot fulfill that function. However, a full analysis of the revised version of *Flower* is beyond the scope of this study. I have prepared a brief table comparing the contents of the two versions; this is printed in the Appendix.[1] Suffice it to say that these last chapters are not of the same quality as the preceding chapters. Even Tseng P'u himself admitted, at the end of his revision, that it was difficult for him to continue the novel because he had to place himself in another time and place.[2]

In Tseng P'u's last years, not only was he unable to write, but even concentrated reading made his heart palpitate. Therefore, he had to give up his literary activities completely. The fact that he was unable to continue his novel hurt him greatly. He had once read about

"Master Chiang reaching the limit of his creativity" (*Chiang lang ts'ai chin*), but he did not understand what that really meant. This popular saying refers to the fifth-century poet Chiang Yen whose poetry began to deteriorate in quality in his later years. Now, in his old age, Tseng P'u suddenly realized the painful meaning of this statement. In his last years in Ch'ang-shu, he had to take up gardening.

In 1934, when his old friend Chang Hung visited Tseng P'u and saw him working in his garden, he was frail and lean, his beard was white. When Tseng saw Chang, he said, "Old friend, I'm planting flowers. This year I have bought some seeds and bulbs from Japan and France. Now I'm just planting them, but next year when you come you shall admire them." After talking about old times, Chang asked about *Flower*. Tseng P'u said that his physical condition did not permit him to continue it, and suggested that Chang take up the task. Chang humbly declined the offer. On June 23, 1935, Tseng P'u died. Several years later, Chang Hung changed his mind and decided to continue the novel. His continuation was serialized in the magazine *Chung-ho yüeh k'an* from 1941 to 1943 and published in book form in late 1943.[3] Chang Hung's work was a true continuation. He began with Chapter XXXI and wrote to Chapter LX, according to the original plan. It was a detailed work that began with Fu Ts'ai-yün's unannounced departure from the Chin household and ended with her liaison with Count von Waldersee after the Boxer Uprising of 1900. Thus, over a period of nearly forty years, from 1903 to 1943, the novel was finally completed after having passed through three hands.

Tseng P'u was a man of indefatigable energy. He was forever young in spirit and single-minded in his devotion to the task at hand. In spite of the chaotic conditions of modern China, Tseng P'u's outlook on life was optimistic. Even though he had many setbacks, he was able to maintain his general enthusiasm. When he set his mind on a project, he mobilized his energies like "a lion going after a rabbit"—completely overwhelming it. Tseng Hsü-pai, Tseng P'u's eldest son, cited these three examples of his father's exuberance: his study of French, mastery of classical Chinese literature, and interest in gardening.

. . . as for learning French, without the help of a teacher, you finally accomplished your goal after ten years of hard work. When you were a young man, you were determined to master Chinese literature. You swore to read through a set of more than 400 volumes of *The Complete Literary Works of the Ancient Period, Three Dynasties, Ch'in, Han, Three Kingdoms, and Six Dynasties Period*. Within three years you actually fulfilled your wish and, thus, laid the foundation of your knowledge of classical Chinese literature. In your later years, when you took up gardening, you would spend the whole day busying yourself in the garden, trimming, breeding, fertilizing, and cultivating. Because the work demanded your personal attention, you forgot all your bodily aches and pains. When night came you continued to read books on gardening, and planned your work for the next day deep into the night. . . . This outflow of enthusiasm we have seen with our own eyes.[4]

It should be mentioned here that *Ch'üan shang-ku san-tai Ch'in Han Liu-ch'ao wen* (The Complete Literary Works of the Ancient Period, Three Dynasties, Ch'in, Han, Three Kingdoms, and Six Dynasties) was a monumental collection of literary prose compiled by the Ch'ing scholar Yen K'o-chün (1762-1843). It contains over twenty thousand literary pieces by 3,497 authors dating from the beginning of Chinese history up to the T'ang Dynasty (618-905). These pieces include edicts, memorials, rhymed prose (*fu*), essays, letters, and epitaphs by poets, statesmen, ministers, emperors, and scholars. The work is in 746 chapters (*chüan*). Tseng P'u's study of this body of writing was not just reading it through, but implied punctuating the text properly (the original text was unpunctuated) and annotating special passages.

His study of French literature has been discussed in Chapter 3.

Because of his personal wealth, social position, and integrity, Tseng P'u showed remarkable moral courage, uprightness, and incorruptibility during his period of political activity from 1911 to 1926. He steered clear of political entanglements and worked unswervingly for the welfare of his province. Tseng Hsü-pai wrote:

When you were the Secretary of the Treasury and Secretary of Administrative Affairs in Kiangsu province, you turned down many underhanded requests and bribes. Your old friends today still tell us about them and publicly praise your incorruptibility. . . Once someone asked you for a position in the tax office, and rented a house with more than ten rooms for you in Shanghai. The house had the finest redwood furniture, curtains, and carpets. There were also antiques and other treasures. . . . But as soon as you arrived and saw them, you burst into anger and immediately ordered a truck to have everything hauled back to its owner. Another time when someone asked you to approve a raise in the price of salt and stuffed a 100,000 dollar (*yüan*) check into your sleeve, your countenance changed on the spot; you upbraided him to his face so that he had no place to hide. . . .[5]

During this period of political chaos and social upheaval in China, it was difficult for an official to know where to place his allegiance except on himself and his loved ones. Even though the rich coastal provinces of central China where the Tseng family lived became the battleground of the seesaw conflicts between the various warlords, Tseng P'u was one of the few unselfish officials who was willing to risk what he had and worked for the interests of his province.

All through his life Tseng P'u felt that he was driven uncontrollably by his emotions and encircled by his ideals. He was a very passionate man. Often his attachment to his ideals would lead him into despair because of their unattainability. But at crucial moments a strong surge of intense emotion pushed him out of despair and drove him onward. In spite of disappointments, Tseng P'u eventually developed an all-encompassing, pantheistic conception of love which became the basis of his being. This outlook was in part determined by his passionate nature, and in part influenced by French Romanticism. He wrote in *Lu Nan-tzu*

Lu Nan-tzu was by nature extremely emotional; therefore, his philosophy of life was based on love. He believed that without love there would not be knowledge; without love there would not be any accomplishments; the formation of the universe is the congealing of love; the movement of life is the continuation of love; color, sound, smell, and taste are the manifestations of love. Heaven and earth are formed from love; states are founded on love; people come into being from love; politics, religion, the virtues, and literature all originate from love.

All his life he pursued love, promoted love, and practiced love, but he did not get love in return; he got mostly hatred. Therefore, recently the foundation of his theory of love was greatly shaken. But there were still two crystallizations of his love which were indestructibly imbedded in his heart: one was the "love of his province," the other was the "love of his daughter." [6]

With the passage of time, Tseng P'u's idealistic theory of love was worn away to only the love for his province and his daughter. In his younger days, he often felt that his life was like a boat on the sea, and the constantly surging waves were his feelings of love. A boat on the sea was actually not controlled by the oars or the rudder, but by the waves of the sea; and his life was controlled by his feelings. Tseng P'u was a man of passion, feeling, and sensitivity, and his philosophy of life was a reflection of these characteristics.

Tseng P'u's literary journey of sixty-three years was an eventful one. He was born and raised in a wealthy scholarly family and had good connections in the official world in Peking. He was prepared to climb the "ladder of success" in the traditional way through the examination system. However, his decision to study French at the T'ung-wen Kuan, after the Sino-Japanese War of 1894-1895, and his subsequent meeting with his mentor in French literature, General Ch'en Chi-t'ung, changed all that. This led to his lifelong involvement with literature—writing, publishing, and translating. His life may be seen as a Chinese writer's self-conscious search for identity in a time of rapid social and political change. His novel *A Flower in an Ocean of Sin* will remain a landmark in Chinese literature, not so much for the influence it had on later writers, but for its marking the end of an era and a literary tradition. It reflected the fin de siècle decadence and revolutionary social aspirations during the last years of the Ch'ing dynasty.

Appendix

The Revised and the Original Editions
of *A Flower in an Ocean of Sin*

This is a brief comparison of the main episodes in the original first six chapters of *Flower* with those of the 1928 revised edition. The remaining eighteen chapters of the original twenty-four are essentially the same as the revised chapters except for minor changes. Therefore, there is no need to compare them. For further detailed studies on the editions of *Flower*, see Wei Shao-ch'ang, *Nieh-hai hua tzu-liao* (Research Materials on *A Flower in an Ocean of Sin*), Torri Hisayasu, "*Nieh-hai hua* no hangi" (Editions of *A Flower in an Ocean of Sin*), also his "*Nieh-hai hua* no shūkai" (The Revision of *A Flower in an Ocean of Sin*).[1]

ORIGINAL	REVISED
Chapter 1	**Chapter I**
An introductory chapter about the Isle of Enslaved Happiness sinking into the Ocean of Sin; the Lover of Freedom, the Sick Man of East Asia, and their sixty-chapter novel.	Same, except for minor changes; a passage in classical prose deleted.
	Headings for the sixty chapters excised.
Chapter 2	
Severe condemnation of the examination system.	Excised.
A maiden's blind infatuation with a *chuang-yüan* and her suicide after marriage because of disappointment.	Excised
	Chapter II
[Beginning of story proper] Introduction of Chin Wen-ch'ing, the new *chuang-yüan* of 1868.	Same

Discussion of the *chuang-yüan* by three gentlemen at a Soochow teahouse (*Ya-chü-yüan*). — Same

Chapter 3

Continuation of the teahouse meeting; discussion of Shanghai. — Same

Introduction of Lu Feng-ju, a friend of Chin Wen-ch'ing, and his forthcoming trip to Shanghai. — Same

A visit to the singing-girl Liang-p'ing-chu by the gentlemen; mention made of Chu-ai-lin. — Same

Arrival of Chin Wen-ch'ing in Shanghai, and his meeting with modernizers. — Same

Lu Feng-ju's arrival in Shanghai, and meeting with Chin Wen-ch'ing; their sightseeing in Shanghai. — Same

Chin Wen-ch'ing's important banquet in Shanghai at I-p'in-hsiang. — Same

Chapter 4   Chapter III

Continuation of the banquet, and Chin Wen-ch'ing's reflections on the *chuang-yüan*. — Same

Chin and Lu's visit to an international flower show. — Same

Chin and Lu's return to Soochow. — Revised and expanded.

Introduction of Ch'en Ch'ien-ch'iu; the origin of the secret societies; and the activities of the revolutionaries. — Revised and moved to Chapter XXIX.

Chapter 5

Continuation of the activities of the revolutionaries; a meeting in Canton.	Moved to Chapter XXIX.
Introduction of Sun Yat-sen.	Moved to Chapter XXIX.

[New material]
Story of the "Four Friends" (*Hai-t'ien ssu yu*): Chin Wen-ch'ing, Ho Chüeh-chai, Ch'ien T'ang-ch'ing, and Ts'ao Kung-fang.
Introduction of a new character, Ts'ao Kung-fang (modelled after Tseng P'u's fatner).
Visit to the singing-girl Chu-ai-lin by the "Four Friends."
Chu-ai-lin's story about Kung Ting-an (modelled after Kung Tzu-chen) and his romance with a poetess.

Chapter IV

Continuation of Kung Ting-an's romance with the poetess, Hsi-lin-ch'un.

Chin Wen-ch'ing and his family's move to Peking; the good life in Peking.	Revised and expanded.

[New material]
Ts'ao Kung-fang's relations with a boy-actor.

Chapter V

Continuation of Ts'ao Kung-fang's relations with the boy-actor.

Old friends' discussion of famous men in Peking.	Revised
An examination of the Hanlin scholars at Pao-ho Palace.	Same
Chin Wen-ch'ing's visit to Chuang Lun-ch'iao, an aspiring destitute scholar.	Same

Chapter 6

Continuation of Chin's visit to Chuang Lun-ch'iao.	Same
Chuang's rise to power and the formation of the "Purification clique" (*Ch'ing-liu tang*).	Same
Discussion of the French in Vietnam.	Same

[New material]
Ts'ao Kung-fang's departure from Peking for home.

Chin Wen-ch'ing's visit to Chuang Shou-hsiang's home; the latter's flirtation with his housekeeper.	Same

Chapter VI

Continuation of Chuang's episode.

Chuang Lun-ch'iao's defeat at the Foochow Arsenal by the French, and his downfall.	Revised and expanded.
Chin Wen-ch'ing's new assignment in Kiangsi.	Same

[New Material]
Chin Wen-ch'ing's attendance at a
recitation of songs about the Black
Flags fighting the French sung by a
Miao girl.

Chin Wen-ch'ing's meeting with   Same
Chu Pao-t'ing in Kiangsi.

Chapter 7   Chapter VII

Continuation of the Chu Pao-t'ing   Same
episode; his romance with a flowerboat girl.

Chapter 7–24   Chapters VII-XXIV

These chapters are essentially the
same with no substantial changes.

Notes and References

Chapter One

1. Lu Nan-tzu is the name of the young man who is the hero of the novel and is modelled on Tseng P'u himself.

2. Tseng P'u, *Lu Nan-tzu: Lien* (Taipei, 1959 reprint), p. 17. *Lu Nan-tzu* was the general title of Tseng P'u's projected six-volume autobiographical cycle of which only the first volume, *Lien* (Love), was completed. Just one chapter of the second volume, *Hun* (Marriage), and two chapters of the sixth volume, *Chan* (War), were written.

3. Lu Hsüan is modelled on Tseng P'u's father, Tseng Chih-chuan, *tzu*, Chün-piao.

4. The office was in fact Department Secretary in the Board of Punishments with the rank of 7b, on the lower end of the official scale of eighteen steps from 9b to 1a.

5. One *mou* is about 0.16 acres.

6. The real name of the garden was Hsü-kuo yüan, one of the famous gardens in Ch'ang-shu.

7. *Lu Nan-tzu: Lien*, pp. 15–16.

8. Tseng P'u gave this tongue-in-cheek description of the *chuang-yüan* in his novel *Nieh-hai hua* (A Flower in an Ocean of Sin—hereafter referred as *Flower*). Obviously, the description was exaggerated, but it was not far from the popular conception: "I think those of you who have not seen an explanation of the *chuang-yüan* do not know its true worth. China is the only nation on earth that has this institution, and there is only one *chuang-yüan* selected once every three years. Only a person who has accumulated generations of merit, who is unmoved in the presence of beautiful women, who has close friendships in the capital, and whose essays are dazzling with elegance is qualified. He is the most outstanding among the immortals and a disciple of the Son of Heaven himself." See Tseng P'u, *Nieh-hai hua* (Taipei, 1966 reprint), p. 5.

9. From a conversation with Tseng Hsü-pai, the eldest son of Tseng P'u, recorded by the author on August 26, 1970, in Taipei, Taiwan.

10. A famous collection of model examination essays entitled *Teng-yin she kao* (Writings of the Teng-yin Society) contains many of Tseng Chih-chuan's essays. Tseng Chih-chuan's many acquaintances at Peking include Weng T'ung-ho, Wang Ming-luan, Hung Chün, and Wu Ta-ch'eng. For

further details on these men, see Arthur W. Hummel, ed., *Eminent Chinese of the Ch'ing Period* (Taipei, 1964 reprint).

11.   *Lu Nan-tzu: Lien*, p. 16.

12.   Ibid., p. 18.

13.   Ibid., p. 19.

14.   For a study of this novel, see Liu Ts'un-yan, *Buddhist and Taoist Influences on Chinese Novels* (Wiesbaden, 1962).

15.   A popularized history attributed to Feng Meng-lung (1520–1601) about the strife and intrigues among the numerous states during the Eastern Chou dynasty (722–221 B.C.).

16.   For an abridged translation of this popular novel, see Arthur Waley, translator, *Monkey* (New York, 1958 reprint). For a complete translation of the first twenty-five chapters, see Anthony C. Yu, translator, *Journey to the West* (Chicago, 1977), Vol. I.

17.   For an abridged translation with paraphrasing, see Lin Tai-i, translator, *Flowers in the Mirror* (Berkeley, 1965).

18.   For a full but not always accurate translation, see Charles Henry Brewitt-Taylor, translator, *Romance of the Three Kingdoms* (Rutland, Vt., 1959 reprint), 2 vols.

19.   For the most recent and most faithful translation of the first sixty chapters, see David Hawkes, translator, *The Story of the Stone* (Baltimore, 1973, 1977), Vols. 1 and 2. For a more readable abridged translation, see Chi-chen Wang, translator, *The Dream of the Red Chamber* (Garden City, N.Y., 1958).

20.   This novel is attributed to the disillusioned scholar Hsia Ching-ch'u (fl. 1750).

21.   This large collectanea of 38 *chüan* was compiled by the Ming scholar Ch'en Jung (fl. 1590).

22.   For a translation of this story, see Wolfgang Bauer and Herbert Franke, translators, *The Golden Casket: Chinese Novellas of Two Millennia* (Baltimore, 1967), pp. 53–66.

23.   For a translation, see Lin Yutang, *The Importance of Understanding* (New York, 1960), pp. 225–28.

24.   For a translation of twenty-three stories from the collection, see Yang Hsien-yi and Gladys Yang, translators, *The Man Who Sold a Ghost* (Peking, 1958), pp. 11–54.

25.   For a translation, see Alfred Forke, *Discourses* (London, 1907).

26.   *Lu Nan-tzu: Lien*, p. 21.

27.   Ibid., p. 22.

28.   Tseng P'u, "Ping-fu jih-chi", (Diary of the Sick man) *Yü-chou feng*, No. 2 (1935), p. 114. *The Romance of the Western Chamber* is a famous drama of passionate love between a scholar and beauty. For a translation, see S.I. Hsiung, *The Romance of the West Chamber* (New York, 1968 reprint).

29.   Tseng Hsü-pai, "Nien-p'u" (Chronological Biography), in Tseng P'u, *Nieh-hai hua*, Vol. 2, Appendix I, p. 2 (paging is not consecutive with the main text).

30.   *Lu Nan-tzu: Lien,* p. 376.
31.   Tseng P'u, "Diary," p. 114.

Chapter Two

1.   Tseng P'u, "Pu Hou-Han shu i-wen chih ping k'ao tzu-hsü" (Preface to the *Bibliographical Treatise* and *Critical Notes*), in *Erh-shih-wu shih hsü-pien* (Supplement to the Twenty-five Histories) (Shanghai: Kai-ming Bookstore, 1934, 1935), Vol. II, pp. 2447–48.
2.   *Lu Nan-tzu: Lien,* pp. 313–14.
3.   Ibid., pp. 317–18.
4.   Chang Chung-li, *The Chinese Gentry: Studies on Their Role in Nineteenth-Century Chinese Society* (Seattle, 1955), p. 11.
5.   Ibid., p. 173f.
6.   Tseng Hsü-pai, "Chronological Biography," p. 3.
7.   This work was published in 1931 by the Chen Mei Shan Company.
8.   Weng T'ung-ho, a native of Ch'ang-shu, Kiangsu, was Grand Tutor to the young Emperor Kuang-hsü and President of the Board of Revenue. For over twenty years, he was one of the most influential men in Peking.
9.   Samuel C. Chu, *Reformer in Modern China: Chang Chien* (New York, 1965), p. 12.
10.   First published in *Ta-wan pao,* June 30, 1935.
11.   Tseng Hsü-pai, "Chronological Biography," p. 3.
12.   *Nieh-hai hua,* p. 30; also see the earlier 1905 edition, *Nieh-hai hua* (Shanghai: Hsiao-shuo lin Company, 1905), pp. 67–68. The later is more complete.
13.   Ibid., p. 37. In the original 1905 edition, this statement was made by T'ang-ch'ing instead of Kung-fang.
14.   For a brief discussion of these works, see *Harvard-Yenching Institute Sinological Index Series,* No. 10, vol. I: *Combined Indices to Twenty Historical Bibliographies* (Taipei, 1966 reprint), pp. 2–3.
15.   Chang Hung, *Hsü Nieh-hai hua* (Continuation of A Flower in an Ocean of Sin) (Taipei, 1964 reprint), p. 4

Chapter Three

1.   A Ying (Ch'ien Hsing-ts'un), comp, *Chia-wu Chung-Jih chan-cheng wen-hsüeh chi* (Collected Writings on the Sino-Japanese War of 1894–95) (Peking: China Book Co., 1958), pp. 495–97. The writings of many others, such as Wen T'ing-shih and Ch'en Chi-t'ung, are also included.
2.   For a translation of this piece, see Cyril Birch, ed., *Anthology of Chinese Literature* (New York, 1965), Vol. I, pp. 167–68.
3.   For further details of the school, see Knight Biggerstaff, *The Earliest Modern Government Schools in China* (Ithaca, 1961), pp. 94–153.
4.   Tseng P'u, "Tseng Meng-p'u hsien-sheng fu Hu Shih-chih hsien-sheng ti hsin" (Tseng P'u's reply to Hu Shih's letter), in *Nieh-hai hua* (Taipei ed.), Appendix II, pp. 18–19 (paging not consecutive with main text).

5.   For these accounts in Weng T'ung-ho's diary, see Weng T'ung-ho, *Weng Wen-kung jih-chi* (The Diary of Weng T'ung-ho) (Shanghai: Commercial Press, 1925 photo-reproduced), Vol. 33, pp. 68a /1–2, 69b /10–70a /1; 30b /5–6.

6.   Tseng P'u, "Letter to Hu Shih," p. 18.

7.   Ibid., pp. 20–21.

8.   Anatole France, *On Life and Letters*, translated by D.B. Stewart (New York, 1922), pp. 76–78.

9.   Tseng P'u, "Letter to Hu Shih," p. 21.

10.   Tsuen-hsuin Tsien, "Western Impact on China Through Translations," *Far Eastern Quarterly*, XIV (1954), pp. 305–27.

11.   Tseng P'u, "Letter to Hu Shih," p. 21.

12.   Chu Hsi-chou, comp., *Lin Ch'in-nan hsüeh hsing p'u chi ssu-chung* (The Life and Works of Mr. Lin Ch'in-nan, Four Records) (Taipei, 1961), Part 3, p. 31.

13.   Ibid., p. 43.

14.   Tseng P'u, "Letter to Hu Shih," p. 21–22.

15.   "Pa-erh-sa-k'o ti hun-yin" (The Story of Balzac's Marriage), in *I-chia-yen* (Shanghai: Chen Mei Shan, n.d.), pp. 1–14.

16.   "Mu-li-ai ti lien-ai shih" (The Loves of Molière), in *I-chia-yen*, p. 13.

17.   *Chen Mei Shan*, Vol. II., No. 4 (1928), an advertisement in that issue, no page number.

18.   Elliot M. Grant, *The Career of Victor Hugo* (Cambridge, 1945), p. 11.

19.   Geoffrey Brereton, *A Short History of French Literature* (Baltimore, 1968), p. 273.

20.   Quoted in James D. Bruner, *Studies in Victor Hugo's Dramatic Characters* (Boston, 1908), 130–31.

21.   *Chin Mei Shan*, Vol. II, No. 4 (1928), advertisement on the back pages.

22.   Ibid.

23.   *Chen Mei Shan*, Vol. VI, No. 6 (1929), advertisement on the back pages.

24.   Donald Fanger, *Dostoevsky and Romantic Realism* (Chicago, 1967), p. 229.

25.   Chow Tse-tsung, *The May Fourth Movement* (Cambridge, Mass., 1960), pp. 285–88.

26.   "Pien-che ti i-tien hsiao i-chien" (The Editor's Humble Opinion), in *I-chia-yen*, p. 11.

27.   Leo Ou-fan Lee, *The Romantic Generation of Modern Chinese Writers* (Cambridge, Mass., 1973), pp. 283–84.

28.   Ting Miao, *Chung-kung wen-i tsung p'i-p'an* (A General Critique of Chinese Communist Art and Literature) (Hong Kong: Ya-chou, 1954), pp. 56–76.

29.   *Lu Nan-tzu: Lien*, pp. 159–60.

30.   Ibid., pp. 367–76.
31.   Frederick Garber, "Self, Society, Value and the Romantic Hero," in Victor Brombert, ed., *The Hero in Literature* (New York, 1969), pp. 213–27.
32.   See C.T. Hsia, *The Classic Chinese Novel: A Critical Introduction* (New York, 1968), pp. 245–297, for a masterful analysis of the novel from many perspectives.
33.   "Pien-che ti i ko chung-shih ti ta-fu" (The Editor's Frank Reply), in *I-chia-yen*, pp. 7–8.
34.   Edward Conze, *Buddhism: Its Essence and Development* (New York, 1959), pp. 107–8.
35.   Tseng P'u, "The Editor's Frank Reply," p. 8.
36.   Ibid.

Chapter Four

1.   Leon Edel, "Literature and Biography," in James Thorpe, ed., *Relations of Literary Study* (New York, 1967), pp. 62–63.
2.   Hu Shih, *Hu Shih wen-ts'un* (Collected Writings of Hu Shih) (Taipei, 1968 rep.), Vol. I, p. 39. This criticism by Hu Shih was written on May 10, 1917, in an exchange of letters with Ch'ien Hsüan-t'ung.
3.   Wu Ching-tzu, *The Scholars*, translated by Gladys Yang and Hsien-yi Yang (Peking, 1957), is China's great satirical novel written in the eighteenth century.
4.   Tseng P'u, "Hsiu-kai hou yao shuo ti chi chü hua" (A Few Words After Revision), in *Nieh-hai hua* (Taipei ed.), p. 3 (paging not consecutive with main text.)
5.   Chin Wen-ch'ing is modelled on the Ch'ing scholar and diplomat Hung Chün (1840–1893), as mentioned in Chapter 2. *Flower* is a roman à clef in which the careful reader can identify actual persons and events of the late Ch'ing period. Tseng P'u used about 280 actual persons in his novel. However, for the purposes of this analysis, it is not necessary to make their identifications. For those interested in the problem see under Chi Kuo-an and Mao Ho-t'ing in the Selected Bibliography.
6.   *Nieh-hai hua* (Taipei ed.), p. 5.
7.   Ibid., p. 15.
8.   Ibid., pp. 74–76.
9.   Ibid., pp. 80–81.
10.   Ibid., pp. 132–33.
11.   Cao Xueqin [Ts'ao Hsüeh-chin] *The Story of the Stone*, Vol. I: *The Golden Days* (Baltimore, 1973), pp. 130–44, translated by David Hawkes.
12.   Wu Ching-tzu, *The Scholars*, pp. 496–503.
13.   *Nieh-hai hua* (1905 ed.), p. 22. This passage was deleted from the revised edition.
14.   *Nieh-hai hua* (Taipei ed.), p. 38.
15.   Ibid., pp. 231–32.

16.   Alvin Kernan, *The Cankered Muse* (New Haven, 1959), pp. 7–8.
17.   Jaroslav Průšek, "The Changing Role of the Narrator in Chinese Novels at the Beginning of the Twentieth Century," *Archiv Orientálni*, 38 (1970), pp. 175. Průšek identifies Hsia-ya-li as Sarah Aizenson, the step-sister of Hessia Helfmann, another nihilist terrorist.
18.   *Nieh-hai hua* (Taipei ed.), p. 89.
19.   Ibid., pp. 95–96.

Chapter Five

1.   Tseng P'u, "Preface," p. 2.
2.   The following are some of the important studies of the characters in *Flower*: The earliest is Ch'iang-tso-chieh-jen's "*Nieh-hai hua* er-shih-ssu hui chung chih jen-wu ku-shih k'ao-cheng," in Tseng P'u, *Nieh-hai hua* (Shanghai, 1916), Appendix, pp. 1–31, 1–14; Chi Kuo-an, "*Nieh-hai hua* jen-wu man-t'an," *Ku-chin*, No. 2728 (1943), pp. 13–20; the most comprehensive is Mao Ho-t'ing's "*Nieh-hai hua* hsien-t'an," *Ku-chin*, Nos. 41–50 (1944). These studies are in the traditional *k'ao-cheng* style; they are meticulous studies of the historical accuracy of the incidents described in the novel. There are also many scattered references to *Flower* in Chiang Jui-ts'ao's *Hsiao-shuo chih-t'an* (Shanghai: Commercial Press, 1936) and *Hsiao-shuo k'ao-cheng* (Taipei: Commercial Press, 1973) and K'ung Ling-ching's *Chung-kuo hsiao-shuo shih liao* (Shanghai: China Book Co., 1962). For continuations and adaptations, see note No. 3.
3.   The following are continuations: Ch'ü Yüan, *Chin-hua meng*; Lu Shih-e, *Hsü Nieh-hai hua*; T'ien-hsiao-sheng, *Pi-hsüeh mu*; and Chang Hung, *Hsü Nieh-hai hua*. The following are dramatic adaptations: T'ien-pao-kung-jen, *Nieh-hai hua*; Hsia Yen, *Sai-chin-hua*.
4.   Hu Shih, *Collected Works*, Vol. I, p. 39.
5.   Ibid.
6.   Lu Hsün, *A Brief History of Chinese Fiction*, translated by Yang Hsien-yi and Gladys Yang (Peking, 1964), p. 372.
7.   Ch'en Tse-kuang. "Cheng-ch'üeh ku-chi *Nieh-hai hua* tsai Chung-kuo chin-tai wen-hsüeh shih shang te ti-wei," *Chung-shan ta hsüeh hsüeh-pao (She-hui k'e-hsüeh)*, No. 3 (Mar., 1956), pp. 39–48. Also in *Ming-Ch'ing hsiao-shuo yen-chiu lun-wen chi* (Peking, 1959), pp. 410–426.
8.   A Ying, "*Nieh-hai hua* tsai wan-Ch'ing wen-hsüeh chung chih ti-wei," in A. Ying, *Hsiao-shuo hsien-t'an* (Shanghai, 1936), pp. 21–27; also see his preface to *Nieh-hai hua* (Peking, 1955). Chang Pi-lai, "Ch'ien-yen," in Tseng P'u, *Nieh-hai hua* (Peking, 1962), pp. 1–10.
9.   Ko Chieh, "Kuan-yü *Nieh-hai hua* te p'ing-chia wen-t'i," *Wen-hsüeh p'ing-lun*, No. 2 (June, 1964), pp. 84–96.
10.   Tseng P'u, "Sai-chin-hua chih sheng-p'ing chi yü yü chih kuan-hsi," in Wei Shao-ch'ang, ed., *Nieh-hai hua tzu-liao* (Shanghai, 1962), p. 40.
11.   A conference on late Ch'ing fiction was first held at the University of

Toronto in 1972. Subsequently, a volume of essays entitled *The Chinese Novel at the Turn of the Century* was compiled and edited by Milena Doleželová-Velingerová and will be published in the near future. Other scholars, notably C. T. Hsia and Jaroslav Průšek, have also done significant work on late Ch'ing novelistic literature.

12. A Ying's *Wan-Ch'ing hsi-ch'ü hsiao-shuo mu* (Shanghai, 1954) gives the most comprehensive survey to date.

13. The most comprehensive study of late Ch'ing fiction is A Ying's *Wan-Ch'ing hsiao-shuo shih*, rev. ed. (Hong Kong, 1966 [1955]).

14. For more extensive discussions, see Milena Doleželová-Velingerová, "The Origins of Modern Chinese Literature," in Merle Goldman, ed., *Modern Chinese Literature in the May Fourth Era* (Cambridge and London, 1977), pp. 17–35; also Milena Doleželová-Velingerová, ed., *The Chinese Novel at the Turn of the Century* (University of Toronto Press, forthcoming).

15. For a brief biographical account of Chin Sung-ts'en, see Wei, *Nieh-hai hua tzu-liao*, p. 134 (n.3).

16. "Chin Sung-ts'en t'an *Nieh-hai hua*," in Wei, *Nieh-hai hua tzu-liao*, p. 146.

17. Wei, *Neih-hai hua tzu-liao*, p, 134 (n.3).

18. Ibid.

19. K'ung Shang-jen, *The Peach Blossom Fan*, translated by Chen Shih-hsiang and Harold Action (Berkeley, Los Angeles, London, 1976).

20. Interview with Tseng Hsü-pai on August 26, 1970, in Taipei, Taiwan.

21. In 1962, a rare thirty-five chapter edition of the novel was published by the China Book Company in Peking.

22. This twenty-four chapter edition was published by Yung-pai Book Company in Shanghai in 1916. This edition can be found in the East Asian Library at the University of California, Berkeley.

23. Jaroslav Průšek, "The Changing Role of the Narrator in Chinese Novels at the Beginning of the Twentieth Century," *Archiv Orientální*, No. 38 (1970), pp. 174–75.

24. The structure of novels like *Flower* is masterfully explored by Milena Doleželová-Velingerová in "The Typology of Plot Structure in late Qing Novels," in Milena Doleželová-Velingerová, ed., *The Chinese Novel at the Turn of the Century* (forthcoming).

25. Liu E, *The Travels of Lao Ts'an*, translated by Harold Shadick (Ithaca, N.Y., 1952), p. 126.

26. *Nieh-hai hua* (Shanghai, 1916), p. 54. This passage has been excised from the revised edition.

Chapter Six

1. Tseng P'u, "Reply to Hu Shih," p. 21.

2. C. T. Hsia, "Yen Fu and Liang Ch'i-ch'ao as Advocates of New

Fiction," in Adele Austin Rickett, ed., *Chinese Approaches to Literature from Confucius to Liang Ch'i-ch'ao* (Princeton, 1977), p. 225.

3. Yen Fu and Hsia Tseng-yu, "Pen-kuan fu-yin shuo-pu yüan-ch'i," in A Ying, comp., *Wan-ch'ing hsiao-shuo ts'ung-ch'ao: Hsiao-shuo hsi-ch'ü yen-chiu chüan* (Collectanea of Late Ch'ing Literature: Materials for the Study of Fiction and Drama) (Peking, 1960), pp. 1–13.

4. Translation by C. T. Hsia, in Adele Rickett, ed., *Chinese Approaches to Literature*, p. 230.

5. Liang Ch'i-ch'ao, "Hsiao-shuo yü ch'ün-chih chih kuan-hsi," in A Ying, comp., *Materials for the Study of Fiction and Drama*, pp. 14–19.

6. Ibid., p. 14.

7. A Ying, comp., *Wan-ch'ing hsiao-shuo hsi-ch'ü mu* (Bibliography of Late Ch'ing Fiction and Drama) (Shanghai, 1957).

8. A Ying, comp., *Wan-Ch'ing wen-i pao-k'an shu-lüeh* (Brief Descriptions of Literary Newspapers and Periodicals of the Late Ch'ing Period) (Shanghai, 1958), pp. 13–16.

9. Ibid., pp. 16–19.

10. Ibid., pp. 25–27.

11. A Ying, comp., *Materials for the Study of Fiction and Drama*, pp. 158–160.

12. Ibid., pp. 156–158.

13. Ibid., p. 159.

14. Ibid., pp. 159–160.

15. Ibid., p. 157.

16. Hsü Nien-tz'u, "Ting-wei nien hsiao-shuo chieh shu-mu tiao-ch'a piao" (A Survey of Novels Published in 1907), *Hsiao-shuo lin*, No. 9 (1908).

17. Tseng P'u, "The Editor's Frank Reply," p. 3.

18. Tseng Hsü-pai, "Chronological Biography," p. 12.

19. Ibid., p. 13.

20. Ibid., pp. 15–16.

21. Chu Shao-wen, "Wo chih Tseng chün Meng-p'u kuan" (The Tseng P'u I Knew), *Yü-chou feng*, No. 2 (1935), p. 105.

22. For a description of the literary controversies of the period, see C.T. Hsia, *A History of Modern Chinese Fiction, 1917–1957* (New York, 1961), pp. 3–111; and Chow Tse-tsung, *The May Fourth Movement: Intellectual Revolution in Modern China* (Cambridge, Mass., 1964), pp. 269–288.

23. Tseng P'u "In the Editor's Humble Opinion," *I-chia-yen*, pp. 1–3.

24. Ibid., pp. 3–4.

25. Ibid., pp. 11–12.

26. Tseng P'u, "Diary," *Yü-chou feng*, No. 2 (1935), p. 112.

27. Bruce Mazlish, "Autobiography and Psycho-Analysis," *Encounter*, XXV, No. 4 (1970), p. 37.

28. Tseng P'u, "Reply to Hu Shih," pp. 21–22.

29. "Humble Opinion," pp. 7–8.

30. "Reply to Hu Shih," p. 24.

31. Tseng Hsü-pai, "Chung-kuo fan-i Ou-Mei tso-p'in ti ch'eng-chi" (Chinese Translations of European and American Literature), *Chen Mei Shan*, II, No. 6 (1928), pp. 1–25.

32. Chao Ching-shen, "E-kuo wen-hsüeh fan-i pien-mu" (A List of Translations of Russian Literature), *Chen Mei Shan*, II, No. 6 (1928), pp. 26–38.

33. Tseng P'u, "Lun Fa-lan-hsi pei-chü yüan-liu" (On the Source of French Tragedy), *Chen Mei Shan*, I, Nos. 1–3, 6 (1927).

34. "Humble Opinion," pp. 13–14.

35. Chow, *The May Fourth Movement*, p. 274.

Chapter Seven

1. See pp. 126–130.

2. "Preface," p. 5.

3. Chang Hung, *Hsü Nieh-hai hua* (A Continuation of a Flower in an Ocean of Sin) (Taipei, 1964 reprint).

4. Tseng Hsü-pai, "K'u fu wen" (A Lament for My Father), *Chuan-chi wen-hsüeh*, Vol. VIII, No. 3 (1966), pp. 29–30. This is a reprint of an essay written in 1935.

5. Ibid., p. 31.

6. "Lu Nan-tzu: Chan," in *Lu Nan-tzu: Lien*, Vol. II, Appendix, pp. 7–8.

Appendix

1. Shanghai, 1962; *Tenri Daigaku gakuhō*, No. 39 (1962), pp. 68–84; *Shin matsu bungaku gengo kenkyū dai kaihō*, No. 2 (1962), pp. 8–32.

Selected Bibliography

PRIMARY SOURCES

"A-fu-lo-ti-te ti k'ao-so" (Study of Aphrodite). *Chen Mei Shan*, 2, No. 5 (1928), 1–38.

"Ch'i-erh ko." Translation of "La Chanson des Gueux" by Jean Richepin. In *I-chia-yen*.

"Ch'iao-chih Sang ti su-sung" (The Case Concerning George Sand). *Chen Mei Shan*, 2, No. 4 (1928), 1–7.

Chiu-shih-san nien. Translation of *Quatre-vingt Treize* by Victor Hugo. N.P.: Yu-cheng Book Co., 1913.

Chung-lou kuai-jen. Translation of *La Esmeralda* by Victor Hugo. Shanghai: Chen Mei Shan Bookstore, 1928.

"Fa-kuo wen-hao Ch'iao-chih Ku-tai-lin lei-sung" (Commemorating the French Literary Master Georges Courteline). *Chen Mei Shan*, 4, No. 5 (1929), 1–28; 5, No. 1 (1930), 1–14.

Fu-jen hsüeh-t'ang. Translations of *L'Ecole des Femmes* by Molière. Shanghai: Chen Mei Shan Bookstore, 1927.

"Fu Liu Wu-hsin nu-shih shu" (Reply to Miss Liu Wu-hsin). *Chen Mei Shan*. 2, No. 5 (1928), 1–13.

"Hsi-la Pi-li-ti ko." Translation of "The Song of Bilitis" by Pierre Louÿs. *Chen Mei Shan*, Nos. 1–3 (1927), 6, 8 (1928).

Hsiang-jih-lo. Translation of *Angelo, Tyran de Padoue* by Victor Hugo. Shanghai: Chen Mei Shan Bookstore, 1930.

"Hsiu-kai hou yao shuo ti chi chü-hua" (A Few Words After Revision). In *Nieh-hai hua*, pp. 1–5. Taipei: World Book Co., 1966. Originally written in 1928.

"Hsü-mu" (Preface to *Lu Nan-tzu*). *Chen Mei Shan*, 1, No. 1 (1927), 1–30.

Hsüeh-t'an meng yüan-pen (Dream of the White T'an Flower). Shanghai: Chen Mei Shan Bookstore, 1931. A drama originally written in 1891.

I-chia-yen (Writings of One Family). Shanghai: Chen Mei Shan Bookstore, n.d.

Jou yü ssu. Translation of *Aphrodite* by Pierre Louÿs. Shanghai: Chen Mei Shan Bookstore, 1929.

"Lan-pang" (Disqualification). *Ta wan-pao* June 29–30, 1935.

"Lei-weng Tu-tai ssu-pu ch'i-shu ti p'i-p'ing" (Criticism of Four Unusual Works by Leon Daudet). *Chen Mei Shan*, 4, No. 2 (1930), 391–399.

"Li-hsien-pin 'Ch'i-erh ko' ti niao-k'an" (A Review of Jean Richepin's "La Chanson des Gueux"). In *I-chia yen*, pp. 1–16.

Lu Nan-tzu: Lien. Taipei: World Book Co., 1959. 2 vols. Originally published serially in the *Chen Mei Shan* magazine from 1927 to 1929; published in book form in 1929.

Lu-k'o-lan-ssu Pao-hsia. Translation of *Lucrèce Borgia* by Victor Hugo. Shanghai: Chen Mei Shan Bookstore, 1927. First published in 1916.

Lü Po-lan. Translation of *Ruy Blas* by Victor Hugo. Shanghai: Chen Mei Shan Bookstore, 1927.

"Lun *Fa-lan-hsi* pei-chü yüan-liu" (On the Origin of French Tragedy). *Chen Mei Shan* 1, Nos. 1–3 (1927).

Ma-ko wang-hou i shih. Translation of *La Reine Margôt* by Alexandre Dumas, *fils. Hsiao-shuo lin*, Nos. 11–12 (1908).

"Min-chung-p'ai hsiao-shuo" (People's Literature). *Chen Mei Shan*, 5, No. 3 (1930), 1–23.

"Mu-li-at ti lien-ai shih" (The Loves of Molière). In *I-chia-yen*.

Nieh-hai hua (*A Flower in an Ocean of Sin*). Shanghai: Hsiao-shuo lin, 1905. 2 vols. In twenty chapters.

Nieh-hai hua. Shanghai: Wang-yün shan-fang, 1916. In twenty-four chapters.

Nieh-hai hua. Taipei: World Book Co., 1966. Revised and expanded edition in thirty chapters.

Nieh-hai hua. Peking: Chung-hua Book Co., 1962. A complete thirty-five chapter edition.

"*Nieh-hai hua* ch'uang-tso chih tung-chi chi kuo-ch'eng" (The Motivation for and Writing of *Nieh-hai hua*). *Nieh-hai hua tzu-liao.* Ed. Wei Shao-ch'ang. Shanghai: China Book Co., 1962. Originally published on November 25–26, 1934, in several Shanghai newspapers.

Nan-tan yü Nai-nung fu-jen. Translation of *Nantas* and *Madame Neigeon* by Emile Zola. Shanghai: Chen Mei Shan Bookstore, 1928.

Ou-na-ni. Translation of *Hernani* by Victor Hugo. Shanghai: Chen Mei Shan Bookstore, 1927.

"Pa-erh-sa-k'o ti hun yin shih" (The Story of Balzac's Marriage). In *I-chia-yen*; also see *Chen Mei Shan* 2, (1928).

"Pien-che i-ko chung-shih ti ta-fu" (The Editor's Frank Reply). In *I-chia-yen*; also see *Chen Mei Shan* 1, No. 4 (1927)

"Pien-che ti i-tien hsiao i-chien" (The Editor's Humble Opinion). In *I-chia-yen*; also see *Chen Mei Shan* 1, No. 1 (1927).

"Ping-fu jih-chi" (The Diary of a Sick Man). *Yü chou feng*, No. 2 (1935), 112–14. The diary was for four days from May 22–25, 1928.

"*Pu Hou-han shu i-wen chih ping k'ao*" (A Historical Bibliography of the Later Han Dynastic History and Critical Notes). In *Erh-shih-wu shih pu-pien*, Vol. II. Shanghai: K'ai-ming shu-tien, 1936. Originally published privately in 1895.

"Sai-chin-hua chih sheng-p'ing chi yü yü chih kuan-hsi" (Sai-chin-hua's Life and Her Relationship with Me). In *Nieh-hai hua tzu-liao*. Ed. Wei Shao-ch'ang. Originally published on November 25–26, 1934, in several Shanghai newspapers.

"Ta Chung-ma chuan." (A Biography of Alexandre Dumas, *père*). *Hsiao-shuo lin*, No. 5 (1907), 1–16.

"T'an-t'an Fa-kuo ch'i-shih wen-hsüeh" (Chats about Literature on the French Knights). *Chen Mei Shan* 2, No. 6 (1928), 1–25.

"Tseng Meng-p'u hsien-sheng fu Hu Shih-chih hsien-sheng te hsin" (Tseng P'u's Reply to Hu Shih's Letter). In *Nieh-hai hua*. Taipei, 1966. Originally written on March 16, 1928.

"Tu Chang Feng yung ko-t'i-shih i wai-kuo shih ti ching-yen" (On Reading About Chang Feng's Experiences of Using Various Verse Forms to Translate Foreign Poetry). In *I-chia-yen*; also see *Chen Mei Shan* 1, Nos. 10–11 (1928).

"Tu-che lun-t'an (fu Tai Wang-tao hsien-sheng shu)" (Readers' Column [Reply to Mr. Tai Wang-tao]). In *I-chia-yen*; also see *Chen Mei Shan* 1, No. 8 (1928).

"Tu-che lun-t'an (fu Wang Shih-ch'iao, Huang Hsü-p'ang, Yüan Hsi shu)" (Readers' Column [Reply to Wang Shih-ch'iao, Huang Hsü-p'ang, and Yüan Hsi]). In *I-chia-yen*; also see *Chen Mei Shan* 3, No. 11 (1928).

"Tu wu chan-lan kuan" (Public Reading Room). *Chen Mei Shan* 2 (1928).

SECONDARY SOURCES

A YING. (Ch'ien Hsing-ts'un), comp. *Chia-wu Chung-Jih chan-cheng wen-hsüeh chi* (A Collection of Writings on the Sino-Japanese War of 1894–95). Peking: China Book Co., 1958.

————. *Fan Mei Hua-kung chin-yüeh wen-hsüeh chi* (A Collection of Writings Opposing the United States' Anti-Chinese Immigration Laws). Peking: China Book Co., 1960.

————. *Hsiao-shuo hsi-chü yen-chiu chüan* (Materials for the Study of Fiction and Drama). Peking: China Book Co., 1960.

————. "*Nieh-hai hua* tsai wan-Ch'ing wen-hsüeh chung chih ti-wei" (The Place of *Nieh-hai hua* in Late Ch'ing Literature). In *Hsiao-shuo hsien-t'an* (Chats on Fiction). Shanghai: Liang-yu t'u-shu yin-shua kung-ssu, 1936.

————. *Wan-Ch'ing hsi-ch'ü hsiao-shuo mu* (Bibliography of Late Ch'ing Drama and Fiction). Shanghai: Wen-i lien-ho ch'u-pan she, 1954.

————. *Wan-Ch'ing hsiao-shuo shih* (History of Late Ch'ing Fiction). 1935. Rev. ed. Hong Kong: T'ai-p'ing Book Co., 1966.

————. *Wan-Ch'ing wen-i pao-k'an shu lüeh* (Brief Descriptions of Literary Newspapers and Periodicals in the Late Ch'ing Period). Shanghai: China Book Co., 1959.

BOORMAN, HOWARD L., ed. *Biographical Dictionary of Republican China*. 4 vols. New York: Columbia Univ. Press, 1967–71.

BRANDAUER, FREDERIC. *Tung Yüeh*. Boston: Twayne Publishers, 1978.

BRERETON, GEOFFREY. *A Short History of French Literature*. Baltimore: Penguin Books, 1968.

BRITTON, ROSWELL. *The Chinese Periodical Press: 1800–1912*. Hong Kong: Kelly and Walsh, 1933.

BRUNER, JAMES. *Studies in Victor Hugo's Dramatic Characters*. Boston: Athenaeum Press, 1908.

CAO XUEGIN [TS'AO HSÜEH-CH'IN]. *The Story of the Stone: Vol. I, The Golden Days; Vol II, The Crab-flower Club*. Translated by David Hawkes. Baltimore, New York: Penguin Books, 1973, 1977. The first two volumes of a projected five-volume complete translation of the famous Chinese novel commonly known as *The Dream of the Red Chamber* [Hung-lou meng].

CH'AN-AN. "*Nieh-hai hua* yü *Hung-t'ien lei*" (On the Relationship between *A Flower in an Ocean of Sin* and *A Peal of Thunder*). *Ku-chin*, Nos. 43/44 (1944), pp. 11–14.

———. "Tseng Meng-p'u han shou nü ti-tzu te i-p'ien chiang-i" (A Letter of Instruction from Tseng P'u to His Female Ward). *Ku-chin*, No. 46 (1944), pp. 25–27.

CHANG CHING-LU, comp. *Chung-kuo chin-tai ch'u-pan shih-liao* (Historical Materials on Publishing in Modern China). 2 vols. Shanghai: China Book Co., 1953–54.

———. *Chung-kuo chin-tai ch'u pan shih-liao pu pien*. (Supplement to Historical Materials on Publishing in Modern China). Shanghai: China Book Co., 1957.

———. *Tsai ch'u-pan chieh erh-shih nien* (Twenty Years in the Publishing World). Hankow: Shanghai tsa-chih kung-ssu, 1938.

CHANG CHUNG-LI. *The Chinese Gentry: Studies on Their Role in Nineteenth-Century Chinese Society*. Seattle: Univ. of Washington Press, 1955.

CHANG HAO. *Liang Ch'i-ch'ao and Intellectual Transition in China 1890–1907*. Cambridge: Harvard Univ. Press, 1971.

CHANG HUNG. *Hsü Nieh-hai hua* (A Continuation of *Nieh-hai hua*). Rpt. Taipei: World Book Co., 1964.

CHANG I-LIN. "Chui-tao Tseng Meng-p'u hsien-sheng" (Grieving over Tseng P'u). *Yü-chou feng*, No. 2 (1935), p. 103.

CHANG, PETER. "The Power Elite: A Literary Image in Late Nineteenth-century China." A Ph.D. Dissertation. New York: New School for Social Research, 1965.

CHANG TE-CH'ANG. *Ch'ing-chi i-ko ching-kuan te sheng-huo* (The Life of a Court Official in the Ch'ing Dynasty). Hong Kong: The Chinese Univ. of Hong Kong, 1970.

Chen Mei Shan (Truth, Beauty, and Goodness). Vols. 1–8 (1927–31). Shanghai, 1927–31.

CH'EN CH'ENG-CHIH. *Sai-chin-hua* (Sai-chin-hua). Taipei: T'ien-hsiang ch'u-pan she, 1967.

CH'EN NAI-CH'IEN. *Ch'ing-tai pei-chüan-wen t'ung-chien* (A Comprehensive Listing of Commemorative Biographies of the Ch'ing Dynasty). Peking: China Book Co., 1959.

CH'EN T'AO-I. "Wu hsin-k'an chung chih Meng-p'u" (The Tseng P'u in My Heart). *Yü-chou feng*, No. 2 (1935), p. 102.

CH'EN TSE-KUANG. "Cheng-ch'üeh ku-chi *Nieh-hai hua* tsai Chung-kuo chin-tai wen-hsüeh chih chung ti ti-wei" (Correct Evaluation of *A Flower in an Ocean of Sin*'s Place in the History of Modern Chinese Literature). *Ming-Ch'ing hsiao-shuo yen-chiu lun-wen chi*, compiled by Chung-kuo yü-wen hsüeh she (Peking: Jen-min wen-hsüeh ch'u pan she, 1959), pp. 410–426.

CH'EN WAN-HSIUNG. "Ts'ung chin-tai ssu-hsiang shih k'an *Nieh-hai hua* te yi-i" (The Meaning of *A Flower in an Ocean of Sin* Seen from Modern Chinese Intellectual History). In *Wen-jen hsiao-shuo yü Chung-kuo wen-hua*. C. T. Hsia, et al., Taipei: Ching tsao wen-hua, 1975), pp. 303–321.

CHENG CHEN-TO. *Chung-kuo su wen-hsüeh shih* (A History of Chinese Popular Literature). Peking: Tso-chia ch'u-pan she, 1954.

————. *Chung-kuo wen-hsüeh yen-chiu* (Studies of Chinese Literature). Rpt. Hong Kong: Ku-wen shu-chü, 1961.

CH'ENG I-CHI. "Nieh-hai hua yen-chiu" (A Study of *A Flower in An Ocean of Sin*). Master's dissertation. Taipei: National Cheng-chi Univ., 1967.

CHI KUO-AN. "*Hsü nieh-hai hua* jen-wu t'an" (On the Characters of *A Continuation of a Flower in an Ocean of Sin*). *Ku-chin*, No. 33 (1943), pp. 1–17; No. 34 (1943), pp. 19–24; No. 35 (1943), pp. 21–24.

————. "*Nieh-hai hua* jen-wu man-t'an" (Chats on the Characters of *A Flower in An Ocean of Sin*). *Ku-chin*, Nos. 27/28 (1943), pp. 13–20; also see *Nieh-hai hua*. Taipei: World Book Co., 1966, Vol. II, Appendix, pp. 1–18.

CHIANG JUI-TS'AO, comp. *Hui-yin hsiao-shuo k'an-cheng* (Studies on Chinese Fiction and Drama). Taipei: Commercial Press, 1975.

CH'IANG-TSO-CHIEH-JEN. "*Nieh-hai-hua* jen-wu ku-shih k'ao-cheng" (Studies on the People and Events in *A Flower in an Ocean of Sin*). In *Hsiao-shuo hsi-ch'ü yen-chiu chüan*; also see *Nieh-hai hua* (Shanghai, 1916), Appendix, pp. 1–31, 1–14.

CHO-HSÜAN. "Tsai t'an *Nieh-hai hua*" (Again on *A Flower in an Ocean of Sin*). *Chung-ho yüeh-k'an* 2, No. 4 (April 1941), pp. 73–77.

————. "T'an *Nieh-hai hua*" (On *A Flower in an Ocean of Sin*). *Chung-ho yüeh-k'an* 2, No. 11 (Jan. 1941), pp. 178–81.

CHOU LI-AN. "Chi *Nieh-hai hua* shuo-kuo chin-ts'un jen-wu" (Remembering the Characters of *A Flower in an Ocean of Sin*). *Ku-chin*, No. 42 (1944), pp. 13–15.

————. "*Nieh-hai hua* jen-wu shih-chia" (On the Family Background of the Characters of *A Flower in an Ocean of Sin*). *Ku-chin*, No. 37 (1943), pp. 20–22.

CHOU MENG-CHUANG. "Hsüeh-ch'uang hsien-hua Sai-chin-hua" (Chatting about Sai-chin-hua by a Snowy Window). *Ku-chin*, No. 25 (1943), pp. 30–32; also see *Nieh-hai hua* (Taipei, 1966), Vol II, Appendix, pp. 19–24.

CHOW TSE-TSUNG. *The May Fourth Movement. Intellectual Revolution in Modern China*. Cambridge: Harvard Univ. Press, 1964.

CHU MEI-SHU. "Liang Ch'i-ch'ao yü hsiao-shuo chieh ko-ming" (Liang Ch'i-ch'ao and the Revolution in Fiction). In *Ming-Ch'ing hsiao-shuo yen-chiu lun-wen chi hsü-pien*, compiled by Chung-kuo yü-wen hsüeh she (Peking: Jen-min wen-hsüeh ch'u pan she, 1971), pp. 512–30.

CHU P'EI-LIEN. *Ch'ing-tai ting-chia lu* (A List of the Three Highest Ranking Graduates of the Metropolitan Examinations in the Ch'ing Dynasty). Taipei: China Book Co., 1968.

CHU, SAMUEL C. *Reformer in Modern China: Chang Chien*. New York: Columbia Univ. Press, 1965.

CHU SHAO-WEN. "Wo chih Tseng chün Meng-p'u kuan" (My View of Tseng Meng-p'u). *Yü-chou feng*, No. 2 (1935), pp. 104–5.

CH'U TUI-CHIH. "Kuan-yü *Hsü nieh-hai hua*" (Regarding *A Continuation of a Flower in an Ocean of Sin*). *Ku-chin*, No. 32 (1943), pp. 1–7.

CLUBB, O. EDMUND. *China and Russia. The Great Game*. New York and London: Columbia Univ. Press, 1971.

CORDIER, HENRI. *Bibliotheca sinica: dictionnaire bibliographique des ouvrages relatifs a l'Empire Chinoise*. 2d ed. rev. (1575–1908). Paris: E. Guilmoto, 1904–08, 4 vols.; supplement (1603–1922), Paris: E. Guilmoto, 1922–24.

CRANE, R. S., ed. *Critics and Criticism*. Abridged ed. Chicago: Univ. of Chicago Press, 1957.

CRUICKSHANK, JOHN, ed. *French Literature and Its Background*. Vol. 4. *The Early Nineteenth Century*. London: Oxford Univ. Press, 1969.

DOLEŽELOVÁ-VELINGEROVÁ, MILENA. "The Origins of Modern Chinese Literature." In *Modern Chinese Literature in the May Fourth Era*, pp. 17–35. Ed., Merle Goldman. Cambridge: Harvard Univ. Press, 1977.

————, ed. *The Chinese Novel at the Turn of the Century* (Univ. of Toronto Press, forthcoming).

EDEL, LEON. *Literary Biography*. Garden City: Doubleday, 1959.

FOOTMAN, DAVID. *The Alexander Conspiracy. A Life of A. I. Zhelyabov*. 1944; rpt. LaSalle, Ill.: Open Court, 1974.

FOWLIE, WALLACE. *French Literature: Its History and Meaning*. Englewood Cliffs, N. J.: Prentice-Hall, 1973.

GEORGE, ALBERT JOSEPH. *The Development of French Romanticism. The Impact of the Industrial Revolution on Literature*. Syracuse, N. Y.: Syracuse Univ. Press, 1955.

GOLDMAN, MERLE, ed. *Modern Chinese Literature in the May Fourth Era.* Cambridge: Harvard Univ. Press, 1977.

GRANT, ELLIOT M. *The Career of Victor Hugo.* Cambridge: Harvard Univ. Press, 1945.

HALSTED, JOHN B., ed. *Romanticism.* New York: Walker, 1969.

HINGLEY, RONALD. *Nihilists. Russian Radicals and Revolutionaries in the Reign of Alexander II (1855–81).* New York: Delacorte Press, 1967.

HO, PING-TI, and TANG TSOU, eds. *China in Crisis,* Vol. I, *China's Heritage and the Communist Political System.* Chicago: Univ. of Chicago Press, 1968.

HOLOCH, DONALD. "A Bourgeois View of the State: Li Boyüan's Novel *The Bureaucrats.*" Ph.D. Dissertation. Ithaca: Cornell Univ., 1975.

HOWE, IRVING. *Politics and the Novel.* Greenwich, Conn.: Fawcett Publications, 1957.

HSIA, CHIH-CH'ING, et al. *Wen-jen hsiao-shuo yü Chung-kuo wen-hua* (The Scholarly Novel and Chinese Culture). Taipei: Ching tsao wen-hua Co., 1975.

HSIA, C. T. *The Classic Chinese Novel.* New York: Columbia Univ. Press, 1968.

———. *A History of Modern Chinese Fiction, 1917–1957.* New Haven, London: Yale Univ. Press, 1961.

———. "*The Travels of Lao Ts'an*: An Exploration of Its Art and Meaning." *Tsing Hua Journal of Chinese Studies,* NS. 7, No. 2 (1969), pp. 40–68.

———. "Yen Fu and Liang Ch'i-ch'ao as Advocates of New Fiction." In *Chinese Approaches to Literature from Confucius to Liang Ch'i-ch'ao.* Ed., Adele Rickett. Princeton: Princeton Univ. Press, 1978. pp. 221–257.

Hsiao-shuo-lin (Forest of Fiction). Nos. 1–12 (1907–1908).

HU SHIH. "Chui-i Tseng Meng-p'u hsien-sheng" (Grieving over Tseng P'u). *Yü-chou feng,* No. 2 (1935), pp. 101–2.

———. *Hu Shih wen-ts'un* (Collected Works of Hu Shih). Vol. I. Taipei: Far East Book Co., 1968.

———. "Wu-shih nien lai Chung-kuo chih wen-hsüeh" (Chinese Literature in the Past Fifty Years). In *Wan-ch'ing wu-shih nien lai chih Chung-kuo, 1872–1921,* pp. 45–67.

HUANG YEN-P'EI. "Chi-nien Tseng P'u" (Commemorating Tseng P'u). *Yü-chou feng,* No. 2 (1935), pp. 103–4.

HUGO, VICTOR. *Dramatic Works of Victor Hugo.* Translated by Frederick L. Slous and Mrs. Newton Crosland. London: George Bell, 1904.

———. *Hernani.* Ed., George McLean Harper. New York: Henry Holt, 1891.

———. *Ninety-Three.* Translated by Mrs. Aline Delano. New York: Athenaeum Society, 1888.

———. *Ruy Blas.* Ed., Herbert F. Collins. New York: St. Martin's Press, 1966.

————. *Theatre Complet.* 2 vols. Paris: Editions Gallimand, 1963.

HUMMEL, ARTHUR W., ed. *Eminent Chinese of the Ch'ing Period.* 1943. Rpt. Taipei: Literature House, 1964.

HUNG YÜAN, comp. *Sai-chin-hua ku-shih* (The Story of Sai-chin-hua). Taipei: Shih-tai t'u-shu kung-ssu, n.d.

JOSEPHSON, MATTHEW. *Zola and His Time.* New York: Macaulay, 1928.

KO CHIEH. "Kuan-yü *Nieh-hai hua* ti p'ing-chia wen-ti" (The Problem of Evaluating *A Flower in an Ocean of Sin*). *Wen-xue ping-lun,* No. 6 (1964), pp. 84–96.

K'UNG LING-CHING, comp. *Chung-kuo hsiao-shuo shih-liao* (Notes on Chinese Fiction). Shanghai: China Book Company, 1962.

K'UNG SHANG-JEN. *The Peach Blossom Fan.* Translated by Chen Shih-hsiang and Harold Action, with the collaboration of Cyril Birch. Berkeley: Univ. of California Press, 1976.

LAPP, JOHN C. *Zola before the Rougon-Macquart.* Toronto: Univ. of Toronto Press, 1964.

LAU, MICHAEL WAI-MAI. "Wu Wo-yao (1866–1910): A Writer of Fiction of the Late Ch'ing Period." Ph.D. Dissertation. Cambridge: Harvard Univ. 1969.

LEE, LEO OU-FAN. *The Romantic Generation of Modern Chinese Writers.* Cambridge: Harvard Univ. Press, 1973.

LEVIN, HARRY. *The Gates of Horn. A Study of Five French Realists.* New York: Oxford Univ. Press, 1963.

LI PEI-TEH. *Tseng Meng-P'u ti wen-hsüeh lü-ch'eng* (The Literary Journey of Tseng P'u). Translated by Meng-chien Ch'en. Taipei: Chuan-chi wen-hsüeh ch'u-pan she, 1978.

LIANG CH'I-CH'AO, et al. *Wan-Ch'ing wu-shih nien lai chih Chung-kuo, 1872–1921* (China in the Past Fifty Years, 1872–1921). Hong Kong: Lung men shu-tien, 1968. Reprint of a number of articles written in 1922 celebrating the fiftieth anniversary of the *Shen-pao* newspaper.

LIU, E. *The Travels of Lao Ts'an.* Translated by Harold Shadick. Ithaca: Cornell Univ. Press, 1952.

LIU, KUANG-CHING. "Nineteenth-century China: The Disintegration of the Old Order and the Impact of the West." In *China in Crisis,* Vol. I, Book I pp. 93–178. *China's Heritage and the Communist Political System.* Edited by Ping-ti Ho and Tang Tsou. Chicago: Univ. of Chicago Press, 1968.

LIU PAN-NUNG, AND SHANG HUNG-K'UEI. *Sai-chin-hua pen-shih* (True Account of Sai-chin-hua). Peiping: Hsin yün tang shu-tien, 1934. Rpt. Hong Kong, 1961. Told by Sai-chin-hua, recorded by Liu Pan-nung and Shang Hung-k'uei.

LIU, WU-CHI. *Su Man-shu.* New York: Twayne Publishers, 1972.

LIU YA-TZU. "Chih Hsü Wei-nan shu" (Letter to Hsü Wei-nan). *Yü-chou feng,* No. 2 (1935), p. 103.

LU HSÜN. *A Brief History of Chinese Fiction.* Translated by Yang Hsien-yi and Gladys Yang. Peking: Foreign Languages Press, 1959.

McALEAVY, HENRY, translator. *That Chinese Woman: The Life of Sai-chin-hua*. New York: Thomas Y. Crowell, 1959.

————. "Tseng P'u and the *Nieh-hai hua*." In *St. Antony Papers* (London: Chatto and Windus, 1960), Vol. VII, pp. 88–137.

MAO HO-T'ING. "*Hsü nieh-hai hua* jen-wu so-t'an" (Chatting about the Characters of *A Continuation of a Flower in an Ocean of Sin*). *Ku-chin*, No. 39 (1944), pp. 1–4.

————. "*Nieh-hai hua* hsien-t'an" (Leisurely Chats on *A Flower in an Ocean of Sin*). *Ku-chin*, No. 42 (1944), pp. 1–5; No. 43 (1944), pp. 1–4; No. 44 (1944), pp. 7–10; No. 45 (1944), pp. 15–17; No. 46 (1944), pp. 10–13; No. 47 (1944), pp. 3–6; No. 48 (1944), pp. 16–19; No. 49 (1944), pp. 23–27; No. 50 (1944), pp. 21–24.

MARCEAU, FELICIEN. *Balzac and His World*. Translated by Derek Coltman. New York: Orion Press, 1966.

MARTIN, W. A. P. *A Cycle of Cathay*. New York: Fleming H. Revell, 1896.

MAUROIS, ANDRÉ. *Victor Hugo and His World*. Translated by Oliver Bernard. London: Thames and Hudson, 1966.

MING-CH'ING HSIAO-SHUO YEN-CHIU LUN-WEN CHI (A Collection of Studies on Ming and Ch'ing Dynasty Fiction). Compiled by Chung-kuo yü-wen hsüeh she. Peking, Jen-min wen-hsüeh ch'u-pan she, 1959.

MOLIÈRE. *Tartuffe and Other Plays by Molière*. Translated by Donald M. Frame. New York: New American Library, 1967.

MU HSIANG-MING. "Meng-p'u hsien-sheng chi-nien ts'e t'i tz'u" (A Poem Commemorating Tseng P'u). *Yü-chou feng*, No. 2 (1935), p. 105.

P'ANG HUNG-WEN, et al., comp. *Ch'ang-Chao ho chih kao* (A Draft of the Combined Gazeteer of Ch'ang-shu and Chao-wen Districts). Block-print of 1904. 50 *chüan*.

PEYRE, HENRI. *Literature and Sincerity*. New Haven: Yale Univ. Press, 1963.

PRICE, DON C. *Russia and the Roots of the Chinese Revolution, 1896–1911*. Cambridge: Harvard Univ. Press, 1974.

PRŮŠEK, JAROSLAV. "Subjectivism and Individualism in Modern Chinese Literature." *Archiv Orientálni*, No. 25 (1957), pp. 261–286.

————. "The Changing Role of the Narrator in Chinese Novels at the Beginning of the Twentieth Century." *Archiv Orientálni*, No. 38 (1970), pp. 169–78.

RICKETT, ADELE, ed. *Chinese Approaches to Literature from Confucius to Liang Ch'i-ch'ao*. Princeton: Princeton Univ. Press, 1978.

RIDGE, GEORGE ROSS. *The Hero in French Romantic Literature*. Athens: Univ. of Georgia Press, 1959.

ROY, DAVID TOD. *Kuo Mo-jo: The Early Years*. Cambridge: Harvard Univ. Press, 1971.

RUH, CHRISTEL. *Das Kuang-ch'ang Hsien-hsing chi. Ein Beispiel für den "Politischen Roman" der angehenden Ch'ing-Zeit*. Bern: Herbert Lang; Frankfurt/M: Peter Lang, 1974.

SHANG HUNG-K'UEI. "Tseng Meng-p'u yü Sai-chin-hua" (Tseng P'u and Sai-chin-hua). *Yü-chou feng*, No. 2 (1935), pp. 76–77.

SHANG YEN-LIU. *Ch'ing-tai k'o-chü k'ao-shih shu-lu* (An Account of the Examination System in the Ch'ing Dynasty). Peking: San-lien Book Co., 1958.

SSU-FANG. "*Nieh-hai hua* k'ao cheng" (Textual Study of *A Flower in an Ocean of Sin*). *Chung-ho yüeh-k'an*, 6, No. 1 (Jan. 1945), pp. 27–45; 6, No. 2 (Feb. 1945), pp. 34–47; 6, No. 3 (April 1945), pp. 25–34.

T'AN PI-AN. *Wan-ch'ing te pai-hua-wen yün-tung* (The Vernacular Movement of the Late Ch'ing). Wuhan: Hupei jen-min ch'u-pan-she, 1956.

TING MAIO. *Chung-kung wen-i tsung p'i-p'an* (General Critique of Chinese Communist Literature). Hong Kong: Ya-chou ch'u-pan she, 1954.

TORRI HISAYASU. "*Nieh-hai hua* no hangi" (Editions of *Nieh-hai hua*). *Tenri Daigaku gakuhō*, No. 39 (1962), pp. 68–84.

————. "*Nieh-hai hua* no shūkai" (Revision of *Nieh-hai hua*). *Shin matsu bungaku gengo kenkyū kai kaihō*, No. 2 (1962), pp. 8–32.

TS'AI YÜAN-P'EI. "Chui-tao Tseng Meng-p'u hsien-sheng" (Grieving over Tseng P'u). *Yü-chou feng*, No. 2 (1935), pp. 99–100.

TSENG HSÜ-PAI. "K'u fu wen" (Weeping for My Father). *Chuan-chi wen-hsüeh*, No. 3 (1966), pp. 29–31.

TURNELL, MARTIN. *The Art of French Fiction*. New York: New Directions Books, 1959.

WAKEMAN, FREDERICK, JR. *The Fall of Imperial China*. London, New York: The Free Press, 1975.

WANG, Y. C. *Chinese Intellectuals and the West: 1872–1949*. Chapel Hill: Univ. of North Carolina Press, 1966.

WEI SHAO-CH'ANG, comp. *Nieh-hai hua tzu-liao* (Research Materials on *A Flower in an Ocean of Sin*). Shanghai: China Book Co., 1962.

————. *Yüan-yang hu-tieh p'ai yen-chiu tzu-liao* (Research Materials on the "Mandarin-duck and Butterfly" Fiction). Shanghai: Wen-i ch'u-pan she, 1962.

WENG T'UNG-HO. *Weng Wen-kung kung jih-chi* (The Diary of Weng T'ung-ho [1830–1904]). Shanghai: Commercial Press, 1925. 40 *ts'e*. Photo reproduction of Weng T'ung-ho's autograph.

WILLIS, DONALD S. "The *Nieh-hai hua* and Its Place in the Late Ch'ing Social Novel of Protest." Ph.D. Dissertation. Seattle: Univ. of Washington, 1951.

WONG, TIMOTHY. *Wu Ching-tzu*. Boston: Twayne Publisher, 1978.

WU HSIAO-JU. "T'an *Nieh-hai hua*" (On *A Flower in an Ocean of Sin*). *Wen-i hsüeh-hsi*, No. 7 (July 1957).

WU MEI. "K'u Meng-p'u hsien-sheng" (Weeping for Tseng Meng-p'u). *Yü-chou feng*, No. 2, 1935, p. 105.

WU WO-YAO. *Hen-hai, T'ung-shih, Chiu ming ch'i yüan* (Sea of Woe, History of Pain, Nine Murders). Taipei: World Book Co., 1968.

————. *Vignettes from the Late Ch'ing; Bizarre Happenings Eyewitnessed over Two Decades*. Translated by Liu Shih-shun. Hong Kong: Chinese Univ. of Hong Kong, 1975.

YANG SHOU-CH'ING. *Chung-kuo ch'u-pan chieh chien-shih* (A Short History of the Chinese Publishing Industry). Shanghai: Yung hsiang press, 1946.

YANG, WINSTON L. Y., PETER LI, and NATHAN K. MAO. *Classical Chinese Fiction. A Guide to Its Study and Appreciation: Essays and Bibliographies*. Boston: G. K. Hall, 1978.

YOSHIKAWA KŌJIRŌ "Tseng P'u no hon-yaku-ron—French bungaku to Chūgoku" (Tseng P'u's Theory of Translation—French Literature and China). *Chūgoku sanbun ron*. Tokyo: Chikuma shobō, 1966.

Yü-Chou Feng (Cosmic Wind), No. 2, 1935.

ZOLA, E´MILE. *The Works of Zola*. New York: Walter J. Black, 1928.

Index

Prepared by Marjorie H. Li

151